Lectionary Journey

Lectionary Journey

Worship Aids for the Christian Year

PAXSON JEANCAKE

Foreword by Scott Sauls

WIPF & STOCK · Eugene, Oregon

LECTIONARY JOURNEY
Worship Aids for the Christian Year

Copyright © 2021 Paxson Jeancake. All rights reserved. Except for brief quotations in critical publications or reviews, no part of this book may be reproduced in any manner without prior written permission from the publisher. Write: Permissions, Wipf and Stock Publishers, 199 W. 8th Ave., Suite 3, Eugene, OR 97401.

Wipf & Stock
An Imprint of Wipf and Stock Publishers
199 W. 8th Ave., Suite 3
Eugene, OR 97401

www.wipfandstock.com

PAPERBACK ISBN: 978-1-6667-1113-4
HARDCOVER ISBN: 978-1-6667-1114-1
EBOOK ISBN: 978-1-6667-1115-8

Scripture quotations are from the New Revised Standard Version Bible, copyright © 1989 National Council of the Churches of Christ in the United States of America. Used by permission. All rights reserved worldwide.

09/28/21

Permission is granted to churches to reprint individual prayers and liturgical texts for worship provided that the following notice is included: Reprinted by permission of Paxson Jeancake from *Lectionary Journey: Worship Aids for the Christian Year*. Copyright 2021.

"Let the word of Christ dwell in you richly."
—Colossians 3:16

Contents

Foreword by Scott Sauls	ix
Preface	xi
Introduction	xv

YEAR A: THE YEAR OF MATTHEW

Advent	2
Christmas	10
Epiphany	18
Lent	40
Easter	58
Season after Pentecost	76

YEAR B: THE YEAR OF MARK

Advent	134
Christmas	142
Epiphany	150
Lent	172
Easter	190
Season after Pentecost	208

YEAR C: THE YEAR OF LUKE

Advent	266
Christmas	274
Epiphany	282
Lent	304
Easter	322
Season after Pentecost	340

Bibliography	397
Subject Index	399
Scripture Index	401

Foreword

The older I get, the less creative I become in my life of worship and prayer. Likewise, the less pressure I feel to "bring my best" to God, as if he was somehow measuring my prayers with a yardstick. I have made this shift because of a later-in-life discovery of the rich tradition of church liturgy, built around the words of Scripture and the rhythms of the church calendar. The benefit of this approach is that formative devotion from the outside (shaped by the words of God) takes the place of innovative prayer from the inside (shaped by the insights of man). This is a wonderful way of ensuring that the whole counsel of God is not only preached from our pulpits, but also through our worship and devotional liturgies.

What Paxson has provided with this volume is a simple, accessible, usable resource for this journey of formation from the outside. I pray that you will benefit from *Lectionary Journey* in the way I know that I will, as well.

SCOTT SAULS
Senior Pastor of Christ Presbyterian Church, Nashville, Tennessee
Author of *Jesus Outside the Lines* and *A Gentle Answer*

Preface

Over the years I have become quite a fan of Johann Sebastian Bach. I deeply enjoy listening to his cantatas and discovering the inspiration behind the music and the text. When Bach moved to Leipzig, Germany, in 1723 and took his position as Thomascantor (with responsibilities at the St. Thomas School and the four city churches), he channelled his energy into writing one cantata each week based on the Lutheran lectionary of his day. He kept up this weekly pace of writing lectionary-based cantatas for several years (1723–25). His goal was to create "a well-regulated church music to the glory of God." Gardiner writes:

> For, from the moment of his official induction as Thomascantor in Leipzig in the early summer of 1723, Bach set off at a pace of weekly church cantata composition so furious that probably no one—not even he, with his extraordinary reserves of creative energy and powers of concentration—could sustain it for more than a couple of years (as indeed he didn't) . . . Such zeal went far beyond any contractual obligation to compose and perform music to adorn the liturgy of the Lutheran church.[1]

The sheer volume of Bach's creative output is astonishing. The wealth of expression he has left for the church and the world is a gift, and it evokes a sense of admiration and respect in me as a worship leader and songwriter. I feel a kindred spirit with Bach, and his influence sparked a desire in me to create an ordered and comprehensive resource for the church based on the lectionary of my day.

In addition to Bach, I have been greatly influenced by Russell Mitman and his book, *Worship in the Shape of Scripture*. Mitman's basic paradigm is "from lectionary to liturgy." Mitman encourages those involved in worship planning to create an "organic liturgy" that flows from the themes and language of Scripture.[2] At a time when biblical literacy is on the decline and the presence of Scripture in our worship services is low, Mitman's paradigm appeared as a timely remedy to these unfortunate situations.

---

1. Gardiner, *Bach*, 288–89.
2. Mitman, *Worship*, 33.

Inspired by both Bach and Mitman, I began to write songs and a weekly blog, offering lectionary-based resources for pastors and worship leaders. This book and other endeavors are the fruit of that inspiration.[3]

Because the content of this resource is based on the Revised Common Lectionary (RCL), it will be of great benefit to you to understand its structure and purpose. A lectionary is simply a collection of readings or selections from the Scriptures, arranged and intended for proclamation during the worship of the people of God.[4]

The RCL was first published in 1992 and contains readings for the Sundays and major festivals over a three-year cycle (Year A, Year B, Year C). The RCL has its roots in Jewish lectionary systems and in early Christian practice. Some of the earliest lectionaries were in use by the fourth century as a way to organize Scripture readings and sermon texts throughout the year.[5]

For each Sunday and for special days in the Christian Year, the RCL assigns a group of four readings: an Old Testament reading (first reading), followed by a psalm of response; a reading from one of the New Testament Epistles (second reading); and a Gospel reading. The RCL's three-year cycle centers Year A in Matthew, Year B in Mark, and Year C in Luke. The Gospel of John is woven throughout the three-year cycle.

Even though it is the last reading, the Gospel reading is the primary or governing text; it is the "hermeneutical key" to understanding the relationship of the other readings. From the First Sunday of Advent to Trinity Sunday of each year, the Old Testament reading is chosen to complement the Gospel reading of the day. The psalm is a response to the first reading and follows its themes. The Epistle is also related to the Gospel reading and gives us insights into the faith and struggles of the early Christian communities.[6]

For the Season after Pentecost, the RCL offers two patterns of readings: the complementary track and the semicontinuous track.[7] Each of these tracks uses the same Epistle and Gospel readings, but the Old Testament and psalm readings are different. In the complementary track, the Old Testament readings are related to the Gospel reading of the day. In the semicontinuous pattern, the emphasis is on reading through an Old Testament book. In both cases, the psalm is chosen as a response to the Old Testament

---

3. *You Keep Hope Alive* is the first collection of songs for the *Lectionary Journey*. It is available on various music platforms.

4. CCT, *Revised Common Lectionary*, 185.

5. Green, *Connections*, xv.

6. Green, *Connections*, xv.

7. *Lectionary Journey* follows the complementary track.

reading.[8] Each new cycle in the RCL begins on the First Sunday of Advent and ends on Christ the King.

The RCL offers a steady diet of Scripture from the Old and New Testaments, follows the cycles and seasons of the Christian Year, and forms us spiritually as we regularly feast on God's word. The goal of this project is to provide Scripture-based worship aids, songs, and devotions for each Sunday in the Christian Year over the three-year lectionary cycle. It is my hope that these resources will be helpful for those involved in planning various elements of corporate worship; however, they can also benefit anyone interested in following a regular pattern of Scripture readings for worship and devotion.

A project like this is never created in a vacuum. I would like to acknowledge and thank those who have been a part of this endeavor in some capacity.

I would like to thank the leadership and congregation of Covenant Church for allowing me the opportunity to incorporate and "field test" these resources in the context of corporate worship.

I would like to thank those who have gone before me, providing resources, inspiration, and insights that have influenced and informed my worship practices and paradigms.

I would like to thank my wife, Allison, and my two daughters, Laura and Mallory, for understanding my need to write and craft this resource for the worshiping church. You are so full of grace and support, each and every day.

Finally, all praise be to our triune God, who relentlessly pursues and restores us. To God alone be the glory.

---

8. Long, *Feasting on the Word*, xi.

Introduction

I will never forget a particular lecture in seminary many years ago. In a course on worship, the professor wrote the number "52" on a white board. He circled it and then stood there for a moment before commenting on its meaning for us. After his dramatic pause, he began to describe the challenge the worship leader faces in planning creative, vibrant, God-honoring worship services, Sunday after Sunday, for fifty-two Sundays every year, not counting Christmas Eve and other occasional services! This is a daunting task for worship planners.

In addition, worship planners are called to steward God's story of redemption (the gospel) through the various elements of worship that we choose each week. Within this task, there is an inherent responsibility of stewarding the word of God.

Regarding the word, I have noticed an interesting dynamic in the life of the church over the years. Ironically, in a tradition that highly values the centrality of the gospel and the word of God, many evangelical churches do not actually have much Scripture woven into the fabric of their worship services. Churches may have Scripture passages printed or projected during the preaching of the word, but that may be the only place where Scripture is read aloud. Additionally, it is either read by the pastor or another leader in the church, not in a participatory way by the congregation as a whole.

Thus, I have become an advocate for more Scripture and more Scripture-based worship elements in the context of corporate worship. This is one of the primary reasons I have found such affinity with the Revised Common Lectionary (RCL).

My passion for crafting lectionary-based worship aids is so that we, the people of God, are singing, praying, being called into worship, and affirming our faith through the word. My desire is for Scripture to be woven *throughout* our corporate worship services, letting its language, narrative, metaphors, themes, teachings, truths, and paradigms form and shape us, week after week.

This desire is captured in the latin phrase *lex orandi, lex credendi* (the law of prayer is the law of belief) which has long been championed in the Christian tradition. As worship planners, it is so important that we understand the relationship between worship and belief.

With this context and these challenges in mind, I believe those involved in worship planning will find this resource to be of benefit in four meaningful ways: as an annual guide for stewarding God's story, as a weekly guide for planning corporate worship, as a steady rhythm for spiritual growth and formation, and as an ecumenical resource that fosters community within the body of Christ.

AN ANNUAL GUIDE FOR STEWARDING GOD'S STORY

As worship planners, we are called to steward God's story. Jesus is at the heart of this story: his birth, life, crucifixion, resurrection, ascension, sending of the Holy Spirit, and future return. In worship, we remember, recall, and appropriate these events and realities. We do this, in part, by following the cycles and seasons of the Christian Year

Our call to steward God's story comes from the various exhortations in Scripture. For example, in Deuteronomy, Moses describes how we are to immerse ourselves in God's story, passing it on at home, at work, and in worship. He wrote to the people of Israel:

> Hear, O Israel: The Lord is our God, the Lord alone. You shall love the Lord your God with all your heart, and with all your soul, and with all your might. Keep these words that I am commanding you today in your heart. Recite them to your children and talk about them when you are at home and when you are away, when you lie down and when you rise. Bind them as a sign on your hand, fix them as an emblem on your forehead, and write them on the doorposts of your house and on your gates (Deuteronomy 6:4–9).

In 2 Kings, Hilkiah, the high priest, found the Book of the Covenant. Finding and restoring the word of the Lord sparked a revival and ushered in a number of reforms through King Josiah.

> The king stood by the pillar and made a covenant before the Lord, to follow the Lord, keeping his commandments, his decrees, and his statutes, with all his heart and all his soul, to perform the words of this covenant that were written in this book. All the people joined in the covenant (2 Kings 23:3).

The psalmists functioned as storytellers in the Old Testament. They often retold all or portions of the story of redemption, spurred on by passages such as this one:

> One generation shall laud your works to another, and shall declare your mighty acts (Psalm 145:4).

In the New Testament, we see how important the Scriptures were to Jesus. Tempted by Satan, Jesus responded by quoting from Deuteronomy:

> One does not live by bread alone, but by every word that comes from the mouth of God (Matthew 4:4).

We also receive various exhortations from the apostle Paul. To the Colossians he wrote:

> Let the word of Christ dwell in you richly; teach and admonish one another in all wisdom; and with gratitude in your hearts sing psalms, hymns, and spiritual songs to God (Colossians 3:16).

To encourage Timothy, a young leader in the church, Paul wrote:

> But as for you, continue in what you have learned and firmly believed, knowing from whom you learned it, and how from childhood you have known the sacred writings that are able to instruct you for salvation through faith in Christ Jesus. All scripture is inspired by God and is useful for teaching, for reproof, for correction, and for training in righteousness, so that everyone who belongs to God may be proficient, equipped for every good work (2 Timothy 3:14–17).

When it comes to stewarding God's story, we should not be motivated by tradition or novelty, but by a *conviction* to immerse our people in the word and to pass this story on, one generation to the next. The liturgical calendar below is a helpful way to visualize this story through the seasons of the Christian Year.

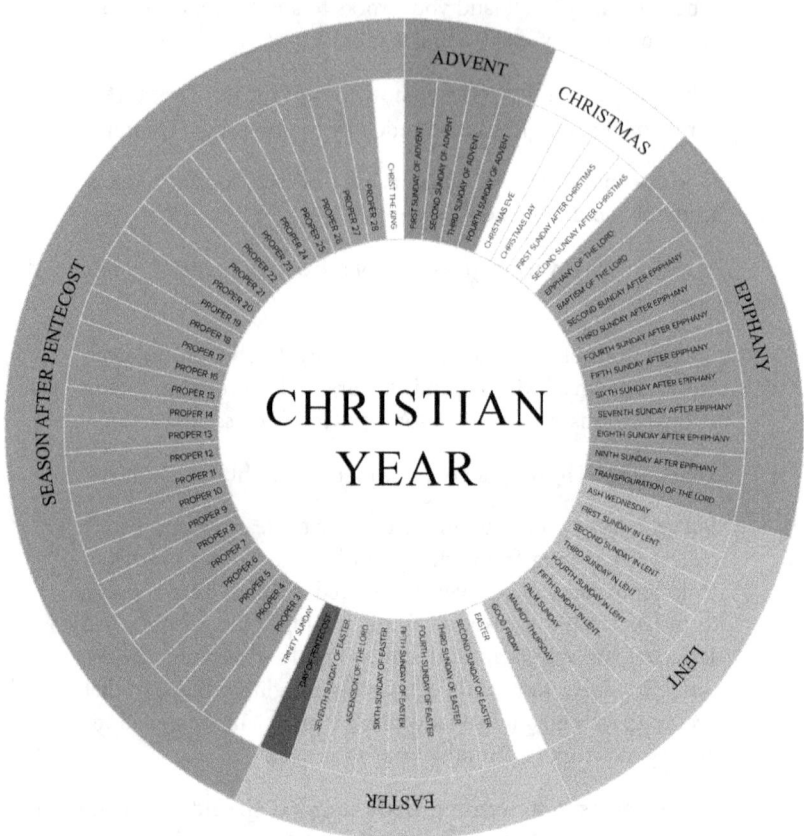

Advent is a time of preparation; a time to remember Christ's first coming and to anticipate his return. At **Christmas** we retell and reorient ourselves around the reality that God put on flesh and walked among us. Throughout **Epiphany** we tell about Christ's manifestation to the world. We recall the Magi who came to see him, his baptism in the Jordan River, and his transfiguration.

Like Advent, **Lent** is a season of preparation. It offers us forty days (not counting Sundays) to orient our lives and prepare for the events of Holy Week and Easter. Thus, we have the opportunity to reflect on those areas of our lives that have too strong a hold on us. We can acknowledge, surrender, and repent over the various idols in our lives: power, addictions, money, control, security.

During Holy Week, we walk through the major events of our redemption. On **Palm Sunday** we sing and shout "Hosanna!" to the King of kings; however, we also remember the irony of this day as Jesus wept over Jerusalem for her blindness and hardness of heart. On **Maundy Thursday**, we remember how Jesus gave us a new mandate to love one another and recall the way he demonstrated this by washing the disciples' feet. We celebrate the Lord's Supper, remembering how Jesus first instituted this meal with the disciples. We walk through the sobering events of his arrest, trial, and crucifixion on **Good Friday**. We rise on **Easter Sunday** to celebrate Christ's resurrection and the hope of new life.

Though it is definitely the forgotten festival among evangelicals, many congregations recognize the **Ascension** (either on a Thursday or the following Sunday) and the reality that Christ is now at the right hand of the Father interceding and advocating for his people. We remember the **Day of Pentecost**, celebrating the coming of the Holy Spirit in power to the church. Pentecost is a time to acknowledge the present ministry of the Holy Spirit who empowers, comforts, fills, and guides us, the people of God.

We celebrate **Trinity Sunday**, acknowledging our worship of one God in three persons. We then enter the long **Season after Pentecost**, celebrating our life in the Spirit as the people of God. As we tell God's story we are formed and transformed, year after year, by the spiritual realities of a living, sanctifying God.

A WEEKLY GUIDE FOR PLANNING CORPORATE WORSHIP

In addition to the annual rhythm of the Christian Year, this resource will be of help in recounting God's story through the weekly rhythm of the RCL. For years, my worship planing involved several independent and sometimes unrelated choices. I found myself spending a lot of time searching for a psalm as a call to worship or for a Scripture reading or a prayer that would flow out of a couple of opening songs. I used to comb through resources looking for an affirmation of faith based on the sermon text for that Sunday.

Lectionary Journey is the fruit of engaging with the Scripture readings for each Sunday (and special services) in the Christian Year and then crafting integrated calls to worship, prayers, and affirmations of faith. With this resource, you will be able to offer your people an integrated and healthy diet of word and prayer without having to spend time each week searching for independent worship elements.

In addition, this resource is of great benefit even if your church does not follow the RCL in its preaching. If your pastor chooses the sermon texts and themes, *Lectionary Journey* still provides you with a weekly structure for utilizing Scripture-based worship aids. And within this structure, there is plenty of room for creativity and spontaneity.

You may choose to incorporate all of the resources for a given Sunday: all four lectionary readings, the call to worship, the prayer, and the affirmation of faith. Alternatively, you may find that it better fits your context to pick and choose from the various resources for a given Sunday.

Often, I will have a vocalist read one of the lectionary readings, and then I will lead the congregation in a corporate prayer of renewal. I will often give some pause for people to make the prayer their own, to silently add their own confessions and petitions; and then I will lead us in an extemporaneous prayer before transitioning into a song of response. Other Sundays, I will choose to emphasize the affirmation of faith.

I contextualize the resources for each Sunday, making choices about what to use and what not to use. There are countless ways that you can make these worship aids your own and tailor them to the culture and context of your church.

A STEADY RHYTHM FOR SPIRITUAL GROWTH AND FORMATION

Although my church does not follow the RCL in its preaching, I have found that by personally engaging with the lectionary readings each week, I am being formed and fed, spiritually. I use these resources not only in worship, but also in family devotions and in my small group. This regular immersion in the word has become an anchor for my faith. It is a rhythmic practice that brings steadiness and stability amidst the various trials and challenges of life. In *Music and the Arts in Christian Worship*, Tom Schwanda writes:

> The strengths of the lectionary actually exert a dynamic, silent force. The more Christians gather around the Scripture, the stronger they grow in Christ. As more pastors and musicians gravitate toward the lectionary approach, there is an increased strength within the church, not just isolated and scattered congregations, but in the church as the body of Christ. While initially this trend may not be easily detected, with time it will disseminate a formative influence much like yeast does to a piece of dough. Anything that can foster broader dialogue with Scripture and about our triune God should be strongly encouraged.[9]

---

9. Webber, *Music and the Arts*, 447.

I have definitely seen this formative influence in my life and in our church. It is my hope and prayer that this resource would be like yeast, exerting a "dynamic, silent force" in the dough of your own heart and congregation. In an age where our attention span is short and our impulse to try something new is so prevalent, this resource offers a steady rhythm for spiritual growth and formation.

AN ECUMENICAL RESOURCE THAT FOSTERS COMMUNITY WITHIN THE BODY OF CHRIST

Finally, *Lectionary Journey* not only serves as an annual and weekly guide for worship and a source of spiritual formation, but it also connects us with the larger body of Christ. Utilizing this resource may encourage you to identify other churches in your local community that follow the RCL. You may explore holding weekly gatherings to brainstorm and share resources for upcoming services.

You may choose to simply educate your own congregation on the global and historic aspects of using a lectionary. You can remind them that as we participate in a prayer of renewal on the Fourth Sunday of Easter, or an affirmation of faith on the Third Sunday of Advent, or in a Scripture reading on Pentecost Sunday, we are proclaiming the gospel along with our brothers and sisters in Christ. We are joining our voices with those around the world and across the centuries who have stewarded God's story each week, engaging with the Scriptures related to the various cycles and seasons of the Christian Year.

It is my prayer that we will steward God's story well in our generation, allowing our hearts, minds, and imaginations to be captured by the saving events and amazing realities of our triune God. In doing so, we are heeding the call to let the word of Christ dwell in us richly.

The Year of Matthew

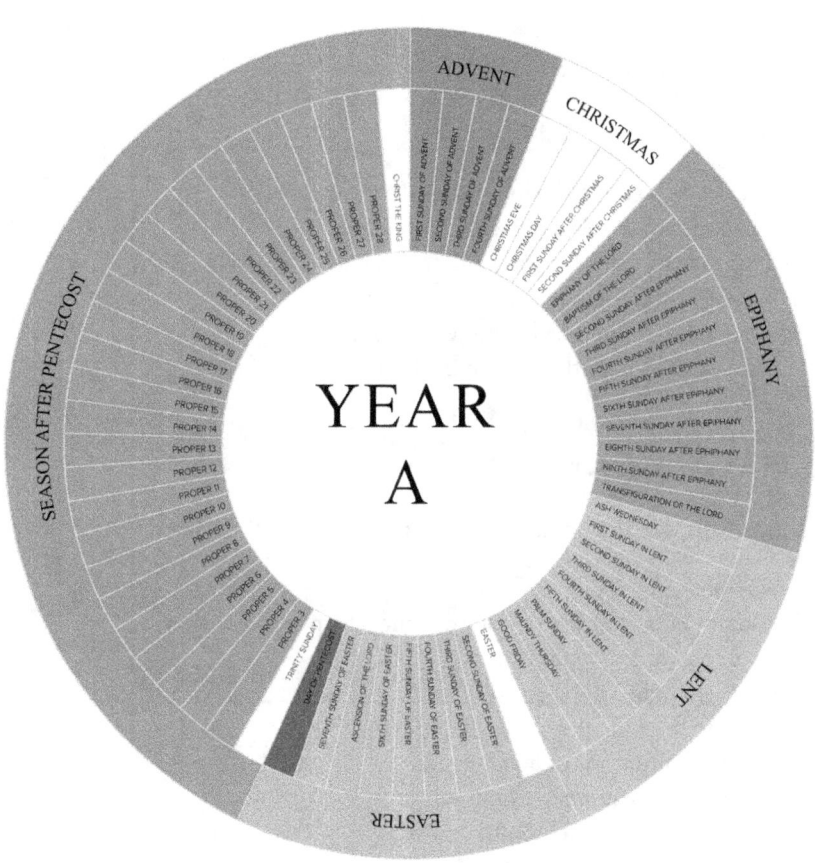

First Sunday of Advent (Year A)

LECTIONARY READINGS

Isaiah 2:1–5
Psalm 122
Romans 13:11–14
Matthew 24:36–44

CALL TO WORSHIP

Isaiah 2:3, 5

Come, let us go up to the mountain of the Lord,
to the house of the God of Jacob;
that he may teach us his ways and that we may walk in his paths.
For out of Zion shall go forth instruction,
and the word of the Lord from Jerusalem.
Come, let us walk in the light of the Lord!

PRAYER OF RENEWAL

Based on Matthew 24:36–37, 44; Romans 13:12–14

Lord Jesus,
we do not know the day or hour of your return.
Keep us awake and ready,
for your coming will be unexpected.
Help us to lay aside the works of darkness
and put on the armor of light.
By your grace, may we live honorably,
making no provision for sinful desires.
In the name of Jesus we pray. Amen.

AFFIRMATION OF FAITH

Based on Romans 13:12–14

How are we to live in light of Christ's return?

We believe we are to lay aside the works of darkness
and put on the armor of light.
We believe we are to live honorably as in the day,
not in reveling and drunkenness,
not in debauchery and licentiousness, not in quarreling and jealousy.
We believe we are to put on the Lord Jesus Christ,
and make no provision for the flesh, to gratify its desires.

Second Sunday of Advent (Year A)

LECTIONARY READINGS

Isaiah 11:1–10
Psalm 72:1–7, 18–19
Romans 15:4–13
Matthew 3:1–12

CALL TO WORSHIP

Psalm 72:18–19

Blessed be the Lord, the God of Israel,
who alone does wondrous things.
Blessed be his glorious name forever;
may his glory fill the whole earth.

PRAYER OF ADORATION

Based on Isaiah 11:1–2, 4, 6–7, 9; Matthew 3:1–3

Lord Jesus,
you are the Root of Jesse upon whom rests
the spirit of wisdom and understanding, the spirit of counsel and might.
You judge the meek and the poor with righteousness and equality.
As it was prophesied, John came as a voice in the wilderness,
calling us to repentance for your kingdom is near.
We long for the fullness of this peaceable kingdom,
when the wolf shall live with the lamb,
and the cub and the calf shall lie down together.
We place our hope in your promises and look forward to the day
when the earth will be full of the knowledge of the Lord.
In the name of Jesus we pray. Amen.

AFFIRMATION OF FAITH

Based on Romans 15:4, 7

What do we believe concerning the Old Testament Scriptures?

We believe that whatever was written in former days was written for our instruction,
so that by steadfastness and by the encouragement of the Scriptures we might have hope.

What do we believe concerning hospitality?

We believe we are to welcome one another,
just as Christ has welcomed us, for the glory of God.

Third Sunday of Advent (Year A)

LECTIONARY READINGS

Isaiah 35:1–10
Psalm 146:5–10
James 5:7–10
Matthew 11:2–11

CALL TO WORSHIP

Psalm 146:5–7

Happy are those whose help is the God of Jacob,
whose hope is in the Lord their God,
who made heaven and earth, the sea, and all that is in them;
who keeps faith forever;
who executes justice for the oppressed;
who gives food to the hungry.

PRAYER OF RENEWAL

Based on James 5:7–10; Matthew 11:2–6

Lord Jesus,
Give us patience as we wait for your return.
Like John, sometimes we doubt and wonder if your promises are true.
Strengthen our hearts and reassure us, for
the blind receive their sight, the lame walk,
the sick are healed, the deaf hear, the dead are raised,
and the poor have good news brought to them.
By your grace, help us not to grumble against one another,
but take the prophets, who spoke in the name of the Lord,
as examples of suffering and patience.
In the name of Jesus we pray. Amen.

AFFIRMATION OF FAITH

Based on Isaiah 35:5–7

What do we believe concerning the coming of the kingdom?

We believe there will be healing and restoration:
the eyes of the blind shall be opened, and the ears of the deaf unstopped.
We believe there will be an overflow of adoration:
the lame shall leap like a deer,
and the tongue of the speechless shall sing for joy.
We believe all of creation will be vibrant and renewed:
waters shall break forth in the wilderness, and streams in the desert;
the burning sand shall become a pool, and the thirsty ground springs of water.

Fourth Sunday of Advent (Year A)

LECTIONARY READINGS

Isaiah 7:10–16
Psalm 80:1–7, 17–19
Romans 1:1–7
Matthew 1:18–25

CALL TO WORSHIP

Psalm 80:1–3

Give ear, O Shepherd of Israel, you who lead Joseph like a flock!
You who are enthroned upon the cherubim, shine forth
before Ephraim and Benjamin and Manasseh.
Stir up your might, and come to save us!
Restore us, O God; let your face shine, that we may be saved.

PRAYER OF RENEWAL

Based on Matthew 1:21–23

Lord Jesus,
We thank you for coming to us,
and for saving us from our sins.
During this Advent season,
we stand in awe and wonder
of the fulfillment of your gospel promise:
"The virgin shall conceive and bear a son,
and they shall name him Emmanuel,"
which means, "God is with us."
Help us to walk in faith,
knowing your mighty presence is among us.
In the name of Jesus we pray. Amen.

AFFIRMATION OF FAITH

Based on Romans 1:1–4

What do we believe concerning the gospel of Jesus Christ?

We believe that the gospel of God was promised
through his prophets in the holy scriptures,
the gospel concerning his Son,
who was descended from David according to the flesh
and was declared to be Son of God with power
according to the spirit of holiness
by resurrection from the dead, Jesus Christ our Lord.

Christmas Eve (Year A)

LECTIONARY READINGS

Isaiah 9:2–7
Psalm 96
Titus 2:11–14
Luke 2:1–20

CALL TO WORSHIP

Isaiah 9:2, 6

The people who walked in darkness have seen a great light;
those who lived in a land of deep darkness—on them light has shined.
For a child has been born for us, a son given to us;
authority rests upon his shoulders; and he is named
Wonderful Counselor, Mighty God, Everlasting Father, Prince of Peace.

PRAYER OF RENEWAL

Based on Luke 2:15–20

Lord Jesus, on this holy night,
fill us with anticipation as we celebrate your birth.
Like the shepherds, may we seek you
with a sense of urgency and joy;
may we glorify and praise you
for your faithfulness and goodness to us.
Your word and your promises are true.
Out of an overflow of joy in our hearts,
help us to share our faith with boldness,
and may all who hear it be amazed by your great deeds.

As we sing and pray and remember the incarnation, like Mary,
we have much to treasure and ponder in our hearts.
You are Immanuel, the God who is with us. Amen.

AFFIRMATION OF FAITH

Based on Titus 2:11–14

What do we believe concerning the birth of Jesus and how we are to await his second coming?

We believe the grace of God has appeared, bringing salvation to all, training us to renounce impiety and worldly passions, and in the present age to live lives that are self-controlled, upright, and godly, while we wait for the blessed hope and the manifestation of the glory of our great God and Savior, Jesus Christ.
We believe Jesus gave himself for us that he might redeem us from all iniquity and purify for himself a people of his own who are zealous for good deeds.

Christmas Day (Year A)

LECTIONARY READINGS

Isaiah 52:7–10
Psalm 98
Hebrews 1:1–12
John 1:1–14

CALL TO WORSHIP

Isaiah 52:7, 9–10

How beautiful upon the mountains are the feet
of the messenger who announces peace,
who brings good news, who announces salvation,
who says to Zion, "Your God reigns."
Break forth together into singing, you ruins of Jerusalem;
for the Lord has comforted his people, he has redeemed Jerusalem.
The Lord has bared his holy arm before the eyes of all the nations;
and all the ends of the earth shall see the salvation of our God.

PRAYER OF ADORATION

Based on John 1:1–5, 9, 14

Lord Jesus,
on this day we celebrate the incarnation;
we remember that though you were born, in time, as a baby,
you were in the beginning as the Word.
You are the light that shines in the darkness,
and you are the true light, which enlightens everyone.
You became flesh and lived among us,

and we have seen your glory,
the glory as of a father's only son, full of grace and truth.
In the name of Jesus we pray. Amen.

AFFIRMATION OF FAITH

Based on Hebrews 1:1–4

What do we believe concerning the way in which God speaks to us today?

We believe that long ago God spoke to our ancestors in many and various ways by the prophets, but in these last days he has spoken to us by a Son, whom he appointed heir of all things, through whom he also created the worlds.
We believe the Son is the reflection of God's glory and the exact imprint of God's very being, and he sustains all things by his powerful word. When he had made purification for sins, he sat down at the right hand of the Majesty on high, having become as much superior to angels as the name he has inherited is more excellent than theirs.

First Sunday after Christmas (Year A)

LECTIONARY READINGS

Isaiah 63:7–9
Psalm 148
Hebrews 2:10–18
Matthew 2:13–23

CALL TO WORSHIP

Psalm 148:1–6

Praise the Lord! Praise the Lord from the heavens;
praise him in the heights! Praise him, all his angels; praise him, all his host!
Praise him, sun and moon; praise him, all you shining stars!
Praise him, you highest heavens, and you waters above the heavens!
Let them praise the name of the Lord,
for he commanded and they were created.
He established them forever and ever;
he fixed their bounds, which cannot be passed.

PRAYER OF ADORATION

Based on Isaiah 63:7–9; Matthew 2:19–23

Redeeming Lord,
we will recount your gracious deeds,
praiseworthy acts, and all that you have done for us.
In all of our distress, it is your presence that saves and comforts us.
You lift us up and carry us; you sustain us all the days our lives.
Like Joseph, you protect us and guide us
though there is evil and warfare all around us.
When we face temptation, you provide a way of escape.

We thank you for your mercy and the abundance of your steadfast love.
In the name of the Father, Son, and Holy Spirit. Amen.

AFFIRMATION OF FAITH

Based on Hebrews 2:10, 17–18

What do we believe concerning Christ as our high priest and the pioneer of our salvation?

We believe it was fitting that God, for whom and through whom all things exist, in bringing many children to glory, should make the pioneer of their salvation perfect through sufferings.
We believe that he had to become like his brothers and sisters in every respect,
so that he might be a merciful and faithful high priest in the service of God, to make a sacrifice of atonement for the sins of the people.
We believe that because he was tested by what he suffered,
he is able to help those who are being tested.

Second Sunday after Christmas (Year A)

LECTIONARY READINGS

Jeremiah 31:7–14
Psalm 147:12–20
Ephesians 1:3–14
John 1:1–18

CALL TO WORSHIP

Jeremiah 31:7, 13

Thus says the Lord: Sing aloud with gladness for Jacob,
and raise shouts for the chief of the nations;
proclaim, give praise, and say,
"Save, O Lord, your people, the remnant of Israel."
Then shall the young women rejoice in the dance,
and the young men and the old shall be merry.
I will turn their mourning into joy,
I will comfort them, and give them gladness for sorrow.

PRAYER OF ADORATION

Based on Ephesians 1:3–5

Our Father,
we praise you for blessing us in Christ
with every spiritual blessing in the heavenly places,
and for choosing us in Christ before the foundation of the world
to be holy and blameless before you in love.
We thank you that you predestined us for adoption
as your children through Jesus Christ,
according to the good pleasure of your will. Amen.

AFFIRMATION OF FAITH

Based on John 1:1–5

What do we believe concerning Christ as the eternal Word?

We believe that in the beginning was the Word,
and the Word was with God, and the Word was God.
We believe that Christ was in the beginning with God
and that all things came into being through him,
and that without him not one thing came into being.
We believe that in him was life, and the life was the light of all people.
We believe the light shines in the darkness, and the darkness did not overcome it.

Epiphany of the Lord (Year A)

LECTIONARY READINGS

Isaiah 60:1–6
Psalm 72:1–7, 10–14
Ephesians 3:1–12
Matthew 2:1–12

CALL TO WORSHIP

Isaiah 60:1–3

Arise, shine; for your light has come,
and the glory of the Lord has risen upon you.
For darkness shall cover the earth, and thick darkness the peoples;
but the Lord will arise upon you, and his glory will appear over you.
Nations shall come to your light, and kings to the brightness of your dawn.

PRAYER OF ADORATION

Based on Matthew 2:1–2, 10–12

Lord Jesus,
during this Epiphany season, we recognize you as King.
Like the wise men from the East, may we seek you,
find you, and be overwhelmed with joy.
By your grace, help us to offer our very lives to you,
and to love you with all of our heart, soul, mind, and strength.
Forsaking the many idols that tempt us, may we bow our knees
before you each day, yielding and surrendering to your grace and mercy.
In the name of Jesus we pray. Amen.

AFFIRMATION OF FAITH

Based on Ephesians 3:5–6, 10–12

What do we believe concerning the mystery of Christ?

We believe that in former generations the mystery of Christ was not made known to humankind, as it has now been revealed to his holy apostles and prophets by the Spirit: that is, the gentiles have become fellow heirs, members of the same body, and sharers in the promise in Christ Jesus through the gospel.

What do we believe concerning the church and the wisdom of God?

We believe that through the church the wisdom of God in its rich variety might now be made known to the rulers and authorities in the heavenly places.
We believe that this was in accordance with the eternal purpose that God has carried out in Christ Jesus our Lord, in whom we have access to God in boldness and confidence through faith in him.

Baptism of the Lord (Year A)

LECTIONARY READINGS

Isaiah 42:1–9
Psalm 29
Acts 10:34–43
Matthew 3:13–17

CALL TO WORSHIP

Psalm 29:1–2

Ascribe to the Lord, O heavenly beings,
ascribe to the Lord glory and strength.
Ascribe to the Lord the glory of his name;
worship the Lord in holy splendor.

PRAYER OF ADORATION

Based on Acts 10:38–40; Isaiah 42:1–3, 5–7

Holy God,
you sent your beloved Son to be baptized;
to be anointed with the Holy Spirit and with power.
We praise you that he was sent to bring forth justice to the nations,
and that he went about doing good and healing all who were oppressed;
as was prophesied: a bruised reed he will not break
and a dimly burning wick he will not quench.
He was put to death, but you raised him on the third day.
We praise you, for you created the heavens and stretched them out;
you spread out the earth and give breath and spirit to the people upon it.
You take us by the hand and keep us as your covenant people;
you open the eyes of the blind, and you set the prisoners free.
We worship and adore you, triune God. Amen.

AFFIRMATION OF FAITH

Based on Matthew 3:13, 16–17

What do we believe concerning the baptism of Jesus?

We believe that Jesus came from Galilee to John at the Jordan, to be baptized by him.
We believe that when Jesus had been baptized,
just as he came up from the water, suddenly the heavens were opened to him and he saw the Spirit of God descending like a dove and alighting on him.
And a voice from heaven said, "This is my Son, the Beloved, with whom I am well pleased."

Second Sunday after Epiphany (Year A)

LECTIONARY READINGS

Isaiah 49:1–7
Psalm 40:1–11
1 Corinthians 1:1–9
John 1:29–42

CALL TO WORSHIP

Psalm 40:1–2

I waited patiently for the Lord; he inclined to me and heard my cry.
He drew me up from the desolate pit,
out of the miry bog, and set my feet upon a rock, making my steps secure.
He put a new song in my mouth, a song of praise to our God.
Many will see and fear, and put their trust in the Lord.

PRAYER OF RENEWAL

Based on 1 Corinthians 1:4–9

Loving Father,
in our own strength, we often fall short,
but you have enriched us in every way,
in speech and knowledge of every kind.
Because of your grace, we are not lacking in any spiritual gift
as we wait for the return of our Lord Jesus Christ.
Though we grow weary, we know you will strengthen us to the end,
so that we may be blameless on the day of our Lord Jesus Christ.
We trust in your faithfulness, O God, and we thank you for calling us
into the fellowship of your Son, Jesus Christ our Lord. Amen.

AFFIRMATION OF FAITH

Based on John 1:29, 32, 34

What do we believe concerning the testimony of John the Baptist?

We believe John saw Jesus coming toward him and declared,
"Here is the Lamb of God who takes away the sin of the world!"
We believe John also testified and said,
"I saw the Spirit descending from heaven like a dove, and it remained on him. And I myself have seen and have testified that this is the Son of God."

Third Sunday after Epiphany (Year A)

LECTIONARY READINGS

Isaiah 9:1–4
Psalm 27:1, 4–9
1 Corinthians 1:10–18
Matthew 4:12–23

CALL TO WORSHIP

Psalm 27:1, 4, 6

The Lord is my light and my salvation; whom shall I fear?
The Lord is the stronghold of my life; of whom shall I be afraid?
One thing I asked of the Lord, that will I seek after:
to live in the house of the Lord all the days of my life,
to behold the beauty of the Lord, and to inquire in his temple.
I will sing and make melody to the Lord.

PRAYER OF RENEWAL

Based on Isaiah 9:2–3; Matthew 4:16, 18–23

Lord Jesus, we thank you for bringing the light of the gospel
into the darkness of our lives. Increase our joy for you
and break the power of enemies and idols that seek to oppress us.
Help us to follow you and your ways each day.
As your disciples, may we be light bearers
in this world, bringing the good news of the kingdom
to family, friends, and neighbors in need.
In the name of the Father, Son, and Holy Spirit. Amen.

AFFIRMATION OF FAITH

Based on 1 Corinthians 1:17–18

What do we believe concerning the ministry of Paul and the cross of Christ?

We believe that Christ did not send Paul to baptize but to proclaim the gospel,
and not with eloquent wisdom, so that the cross of Christ might not be emptied of its power.
We believe the message about the cross is foolishness to those who are perishing, but to us who are being saved it is the power of God.

Fourth Sunday after Epiphany (Year A)

LECTIONARY READINGS

Micah 6:1–8
Psalm 15
1 Corinthians 1:18–31
Matthew 5:1–12

CALL TO WORSHIP

Micah 6:6, 8

With what shall I come before the Lord, and bow myself before God on high?
He has told you, O mortal, what is good; and what does the Lord require of you but to do justice, and to love kindness, and to walk humbly with your God?

PRAYER OF RENEWAL

Based on Matthew 5:3–12

Holy God,
your ways are so different from our ways.
Help us, by your grace, to live the kind of life
that reveals the values of your kingdom.
Help us to find your blessing through a poverty in spirit;
through meekness and mourning.
May we hunger and thirst for righteousness;
may we seek to be merciful, pure in heart
and peacemaking in our relationships.
May we know your presence and reward
through persecution and false accusation.
We pray for this kind of life in the name of
the Father, the Son, and the Holy Spirit. Amen.

AFFIRMATION OF FAITH

Based on 1 Corinthians 1:23–25, 27–29

What do we believe concerning the message of the gospel?

We believe in Christ crucified, a stumbling block to Jews and foolishness to gentiles, but to those who are the called, both Jews and Greeks,
Christ the power of God and the wisdom of God.
We believe that God's foolishness is wiser than human wisdom,
and God's weakness is stronger than human strength.
We believe that God chose what is foolish in the world to shame the wise; God chose what is weak in the world to shame the strong; God chose what is low and despised in the world, to reduce to nothing things that are, so that no one might boast in the presence of God.

Fifth Sunday after Epiphany (Year A)

LECTIONARY READINGS

Isaiah 58:1–12
Psalm 112:1–10
1 Corinthians 2:1–16
Matthew 5:13–20

CALL TO WORSHIP

Psalm 112:1

Praise the Lord!
Happy are those who fear the Lord,
who greatly delight in his commandments.

PRAYER OF RENEWAL

Based on Matthew 5:14–20; Isaiah 58:6–7

Merciful God,
as your people, may our light shine before others,
so that they may see the fruit of the Spirit
in our lives and give you glory.
Help us to live righteously in this world,
bringing the gospel, in word and in deed,
to those who are in bondage;
to those who are homeless and poor;
to those who suffering physically, spiritually, and emotionally.
In the name of Jesus we pray. Amen.

AFFIRMATION OF FAITH

Based on 1 Corinthians 2:11–13

What do we believe concerning the Spirit and our understanding of God?

We believe that no one comprehends what is truly God's except the Spirit of God.
We believe that we have received not the spirit of the world, but the Spirit that is from God,
so that we may understand the gifts bestowed on us by God.
We believe that we speak of these things in words not taught by human wisdom
but taught by the Spirit, interpreting spiritual things to those who are spiritual.

Sixth Sunday after Epiphany (Year A)

LECTIONARY READINGS

Deuteronomy 30:15–20
Psalm 119:1–8
1 Corinthians 3:1–9
Matthew 5:21–37

CALL TO WORSHIP

Psalm 119:1–3, 7–8

Happy are those whose way is blameless, who walk in the law of the Lord.
Happy are those who keep his decrees, who seek him with their whole heart,
who also do no wrong, but walk in his ways.
I will praise you with an upright heart,
when I learn your righteous ordinances.
I will observe your statutes; do not utterly forsake me.

PRAYER OF RENEWAL

Based on Matthew 5:21–37

Lord Jesus,
we confess that your standard is much higher than ours,
and that we battle the flesh in more subtle ways than we often realize.
Your word tells us that we not only sin when we murder,
but when we insult or harbor anger towards another person,
we have committed murder in our heart.
Your word tells us that we not only sin when we commit adultery,
but when we look with lust at another person, we have committed adultery in our heart.
Your word tells us that we not only sin when we fail to keep our vows to the Lord,

but when we fail to keep our word with anyone, we have sworn falsely before you.
Help us to have integrity with our vows and commitments.
Transform our hearts, O Lord, by the power of the Holy Spirit;
may we seek you with our whole heart.
In the name of Jesus we pray. Amen.

AFFIRMATION OF FAITH

Based on 1 Corinthians 3:7–8

What do we believe concerning the work of vocational evangelists?

We believe that neither the one who plants nor the one who waters is anything, but only God who gives the growth.
We believe that the one who plants and the one who waters have a common purpose, and each will receive wages according to the labor of each.

Seventh Sunday after Epiphany (Year A)

LECTIONARY READINGS

Leviticus 19:1–2, 9–18
Psalm 119:33–40
1 Corinthians 3:10–11, 16–23
Matthew 5:38–48

CALL TO WORSHIP

Psalm 119:33–37

Teach me, O Lord, the way of your statutes, and I will observe it to the end.
Give me understanding, that I may keep your law and observe it with my whole heart.
Lead me in the path of your commandments, for I delight in it.
Turn my heart to your decrees, and not to selfish gain.
Turn my eyes from looking at vanities; give me life in your ways.

PRAYER OF RENEWAL

Based on Matthew 5:40–44

Merciful God,
help us to be gracious to others
as you have been gracious to us.
Give us hearts that go out of our way
to serve and minister to someone else.
May the Spirit be at work in us,
allowing us to love even our enemies,
and to pray for those who persecute us.
Refine us and sanctify us, O Lord,
that we would shine as bright lights in this broken world.
In the name of Jesus we pray. Amen.

AFFIRMATION OF FAITH

Based on 1 Corinthians 3:16–17

What do we believe concerning the church as God's temple?

We believe that we are God's temple and that God's Spirit dwells in us,
the body of believers, personally and corporately.
We believe that if anyone destroys God's temple, God will destroy that person.
For God's temple is holy, and we are that temple.

Eighth Sunday after Epiphany (Year A)

LECTIONARY READINGS

Isaiah 49:8–16a
Psalm 131
1 Corinthians 4:1–5
Matthew 6:24–34

CALL TO WORSHIP

Psalm 131

O Lord, my heart is not lifted up, my eyes are not raised too high;
I do not occupy myself with things too great and too marvelous for me.
But I have calmed and quieted my soul,
like a weaned child with its mother;
my soul is like the weaned child that is with me.
O Israel, hope in the Lord from this time on and forevermore.

PRAYER OF RENEWAL

Based on Matthew 6:25–34

Lord Jesus, our hearts long for rest.
Help us not to worry about our life:
what we will eat or what we will drink,
or about our bodies, what we will wear.
We know that you care for all of your creation,
providing food and nourishment for all living things.
When we become anxious and fearful, by your grace,
help us to trust in your provision for each new day.
May we strive first for your kingdom and your righteousness,
knowing that all of these earthly concerns will be given to us as well.
In the name of Jesus we pray. Amen.

AFFIRMATION OF FAITH

Based on 1 Corinthians 4:1–2

What do we believe concerning the ministry of the apostles?

We believe we are to think of the apostles as servants
of Christ and stewards of God's mysteries.
We believe that it is required of stewards that they be found trustworthy.

Ninth Sunday after Epiphany (Year A)

LECTIONARY READINGS

Deuteronomy 11:18–21, 26–28
Psalm 31:1–5, 19–24
Romans 1:16–17; 3:22b–31
Matthew 7:21–29

CALL TO WORSHIP

Psalm 31:1–2, 19

In you, O Lord, I seek refuge; do not let me ever be put to shame;
in your righteousness deliver me. Incline your ear to me; rescue me speedily.
Be a rock of refuge for me, a strong fortress to save me.
O how abundant is your goodness that you have laid up for those who fear you,
and accomplished for those who take refuge in you, in the sight of everyone!

PRAYER OF RENEWAL

Based on Deuteronomy 11:18–21; Matthew 7:24–27

Lord Jesus, help us to put your word in our heart and soul,
feasting on it in such a way that it would nourish us and fill us.
May we be diligent to teach our children about your mighty deeds,
talking about them when we are at home and when we are away,
when we lie down and when we rise.
By your grace, let the truth of the gospel bring abundant blessing upon our lives. Forgive us when we foolishly neglect your word and commandments, finding ourselves vulnerable to temptation; lacking in faith, hope, and love; and quenching our fellowship with the Holy Spirit.

For our desire is to be like a wise man who built his house on rock, able to withstand the storms and trials of this life, and drawing ever closer to you. In the name of Jesus we pray.

AFFIRMATION OF FAITH

Based on Romans 1:16-17; 3:27-28, 30

What do we believe concerning the gospel?

We believe the gospel is the power of God for salvation to everyone who has faith, to the Jew first and also to the Greek. For in it the righteousness of God is revealed through faith for faith; as it is written, "The one who is righteous will live by faith."
We believe there is no room for boasting for we hold that a person is justified by faith apart from works prescribed by the law. God will justify the circumcised on the ground of faith and the uncircumcised through that same faith.

Transfiguration of the Lord (Year A)

LECTIONARY READINGS

Exodus 24:12–18
Psalm 2
2 Peter 1:16–21
Matthew 17:1–9

CALL TO WORSHIP

Psalm 2:10–11

Now therefore, O kings, be wise; be warned, O rulers of the earth.
Serve the Lord with fear, with trembling kiss his feet,
or he will be angry, and you will perish in the way;
for his wrath is quickly kindled.
Happy are all who take refuge in him.

PRAYER OF ADORATION

Based on Psalm 2; 2 Peter 1:19

Lord Jesus,
you are the beloved Son of God who reigns from heaven.
All the nations of the earth are subject to you; you rule over all.
Help us to be attentive to the message of your glory and salvation;
may it influence our lives until the day of your return. Amen.

AFFIRMATION OF FAITH

Based on Matthew 17:1–3, 5

What do we believe concerning the transfiguration of the Lord?

We believe that Jesus took with him Peter and James and his brother John
and led them up a high mountain, by themselves.
We believe that he was transfigured before them,
and his face shone like the sun, and his clothes became dazzling white.
We believe that there appeared to them Moses and Elijah, talking with him.
We believe that a bright cloud overshadowed them, and from the cloud a voice said,
"This is my Son, the Beloved; with him I am well pleased; listen to him!"

Ash Wednesday (Year A)

LECTIONARY READINGS

Joel 2:1–2, 12–17
Psalm 51:1–17
2 Corinthians 5:20b–6:10
Matthew 6:1–6, 16–21

CALL TO WORSHIP

Joel 2:15–16

Blow the trumpet in Zion; sanctify a fast;
call a solemn assembly; gather the people.
Sanctify the congregation; assemble the aged;
gather the children, even infants at the breast.
Let the bridegroom leave his room, and the bride her canopy.

PRAYER OF RENEWAL

Based on Psalm 51:1–2, 6–12

Have mercy on us, O God, according to your steadfast love;
according to your abundant mercy blot out our transgressions.
Wash us thoroughly from our iniquity, and cleanse us from our sin.
You desire truth in the inward being;
therefore teach us wisdom in our secret heart.
Purge us with hyssop, and we shall be clean;
wash us, and we shall be whiter than snow.
Let us hear joy and gladness; let the bones that you have crushed rejoice.
Hide your face from our sins, and blot out all our iniquities.
Create in us a clean heart, O God, and put a new and right spirit within us.
Do not cast us away from your presence, and do not take your holy spirit from us.

Restore to us the joy of your salvation, and sustain in us a willing spirit. Amen.

AFFIRMATION OF FAITH

Based on Matthew 6:5–6, 16–18

What do we believe concerning prayer and fasting?

We believe that whenever we pray, we are not to be like the hypocrites; for they love to stand and pray in the synagogues and at the street corners, so that they may be seen by others. But whenever we pray, we are to go into our room and shut the door and pray to our Father who is in secret; and our Father who sees in secret will reward us.

We believe that whenever we fast, we are not to look dismal, like the hypocrites, for they disfigure their faces so as to show others that they are fasting. But when we fast, we are to clean up and wash our face, so that our fasting may be seen not by others but by our Father who is in secret; and our Father who sees in secret will reward us.

First Sunday in Lent (Year A)

LECTIONARY READINGS

Genesis 2:15–17; 3:1–7
Psalm 32
Romans 5:12–19
Matthew 4:1–11

CALL TO WORSHIP

Psalm 32:7, 11

You are a hiding place for me;
you preserve me from trouble;
you surround me with glad cries of deliverance.
Be glad in the Lord and rejoice, O righteous,
and shout for joy, all you upright in heart.

PRAYER OF RENEWAL

Based on Genesis 3:1–7; Psalm 32:3–5; Matthew 4:1–11

Lord Jesus,
we acknowledge that we often try to hide our sin from you.
Naked and ashamed, our souls grow weary and heavy
and our bodies waste away
while we keep our transgressions to ourselves.
Help us to more readily confess our hearts before you,
finding the forgiveness and healing we truly desire.
May we resist the temptations of the evil one,
protecting ourselves through the power of the Spirit
and the strength of your word.
In the name of Jesus we pray. Amen.

AFFIRMATION OF FAITH

Based on Romans 5:18–19

What do we believe concerning the sin of Adam and the righteousness of Christ?

We believe that just as Adam's trespass led to condemnation for all,
so Christ's act of righteousness leads to justification and life for all.
For just as by the one man's disobedience the many were made sinners,
so by the one man's obedience the many will be made righteous.

Second Sunday in Lent (Year A)

LECTIONARY READINGS

Genesis 12:1–4a
Psalm 121
Romans 4:1–5, 13–17
John 3:1–17

CALL TO WORSHIP

Psalm 121:1–2, 7–8

I lift up my eyes to the hills—
from where will my help come?
My help comes from the Lord, who made heaven and earth.
The Lord will keep you from all evil; he will keep your life.
The Lord will keep your going out and your coming in
from this time on and forevermore.

PRAYER OF RENEWAL

Based on Romans 4:16; John 3:5, 16

Almighty God,
you are the one who keeps his covenant
to a thousand generations.
By faith, we believe the promise
you made to Abraham long ago.
By grace, we receive all the benefits of that promise
as the spiritual children of Abraham.
As those born of water and Spirit,
we trust in you to guide us and give us eternal life.
In the name of Jesus we pray. Amen.

AFFIRMATION OF FAITH

Based on John 3:5–8

What do we believe concerning being born again?

We believe Jesus said that we must be born again, for no one can enter
the kingdom of God without being born of water and Spirit.
We believe that what is born of the flesh is flesh,
and what is born of the Spirit is spirit.
The wind blows where it chooses, and we hear the sound of it,
but we do not know where it comes from or where it goes.
We believe that it is the same with everyone who is born of the Spirit.

Third Sunday in Lent (Year A)

LECTIONARY READINGS

Exodus 17:1–7
Psalm 95
Romans 5:1–11
John 4:5–42

CALL TO WORSHIP

Psalm 95:1–2

O come, let us sing to the Lord;
let us make a joyful noise to the rock of our salvation!
Let us come into his presence with thanksgiving;
let us make a joyful noise to him with songs of praise!

PRAYER OF RENEWAL

Based on John 4:5–42

Lord Jesus,
we come to you with thirsty souls.
Like the woman at the well,
we are full of pride and false assumptions about you.
Though our stories are messy and our needs are great,
we often remain at a distance from you.
Grant us joy and peace, for you know all we have ever done,
yet you love us with an unfailing love.
Give us boldness to share this good news,
from hearts overflowing with gratitude,
to those around us that need your grace.
In the name of Jesus we pray. Amen.

AFFIRMATION OF FAITH

Based on Romans 5:1–5

What do we believe concerning justification by faith?

We believe that since we are justified by faith, we have peace with God through our Lord Jesus Christ, through whom we have obtained access to this grace in which we stand.

What do we believe regarding suffering?

We believe that we can boast in our sufferings,
knowing that suffering produces endurance,
and endurance produces character, and character produces hope,
and hope does not disappoint us, because God's love has been poured into our hearts through the Holy Spirit who has been given to us.

Fourth Sunday in Lent (Year A)

LECTIONARY READINGS

1 Samuel 16:1–13
Psalm 23
Ephesians 5:8–14
John 9:1–41

CALL TO WORSHIP

Psalm 23:1–3

The Lord is my shepherd, I shall not want.
He makes me lie down in green pastures;
he leads me beside still waters; he restores my soul.
He leads me in right paths for his name's sake.

PRAYER OF ADORATION

Based on Psalm 23; 1 Samuel 16:7; John 9:25

Good Shepherd,
we rejoice in you for you restore our souls.
You grant us safety and peace
and protect us from our enemies.
We delight in you for your goodness and mercy
follow us all the days of our lives.
We praise you for you do not see us
by our outward appearances; you look at our hearts.
By your grace, we who were once blind, now see.
In the name of Jesus we pray. Amen.

AFFIRMATION OF FAITH

Based on Ephesians 5:8–11

How are we to live as followers of Christ?

We believe we are to live as children of light—
for the fruit of the light is found in all that is good and right and true.
We believe we are to try to find out what is pleasing to the Lord
and take no part in the unfruitful works of darkness, but instead expose them.

Fifth Sunday in Lent (Year A)

LECTIONARY READINGS

Ezekiel 37:1–14
Psalm 130
Romans 8:6–11
John 11:1–45

CALL TO WORSHIP

Psalm 130:5–6

I wait for the Lord, my soul waits,
and in his word I hope.
My soul waits for the Lord
more than those who watch for the morning.

PRAYER OF RENEWAL

Based on John 11:25–26; Ezekiel 37:1–14; Romans 8:6

Lord Jesus,
you are the resurrection and the life.
Like the valley of dry bones,
you breathe life into your people,
filling us with the breath of your Spirit.
Help us to set our minds,
not on the flesh, which is death,
but on the Spirit, who is life and peace.
In the name of Jesus we pray. Amen.

AFFIRMATION OF FAITH

Based on Romans 8:6–10

What do we believe concerning the flesh and the Spirit?

We believe that to set the mind on the flesh is death,
but to set the mind on the Spirit is life and peace.
We believe that the mind that is set on the flesh is hostile to God;
it does not submit to God's law—indeed it cannot,
and those who are in the flesh cannot please God.
We believe that if Christ is in us, though the body is dead because of sin,
the Spirit is life because of righteousness.

Palm Sunday (Year A)

LECTIONARY READINGS

Psalm 118:1–2, 19–29
Matthew 21:1–11

CALL TO WORSHIP

Psalm 118:26, 28–29

Blessed is the one who comes in the name of the Lord.
We bless you from the house of the Lord.
You are my God, and I will give thanks to you;
you are my God, I will extol you.
O give thanks to the Lord, for he is good,
for his steadfast love endures forever.

PRAYER OF ADORATION

Based on Matthew 21:5, 11

Lord Jesus,
we praise you as our Prophet,
who speaks and who is the Word
of life for hungry souls.
We worship you as our Priest,
who rode into Jerusalem to offer
and to be the atoning sacrifice for our sins.
We adore you as our King,
who came to save us and protect us as your own. Amen.

AFFIRMATION OF FAITH

Based on Matthew 21:6–9

What do we believe concerning Jesus' triumphal entry into Jerusalem?

We believe the disciples brought a donkey and a colt,
and put their cloaks on them, and that Jesus sat on them.
We believe a very large crowd spread their cloaks on the road,
and others cut branches from the trees and spread them on the road.
We believe the crowds that went ahead of him and that followed were shouting,
"Hosanna to the Son of David!
Blessed is the one who comes in the name of the Lord!
Hosanna in the highest heaven!"

Maundy Thursday (Year A)

LECTIONARY READINGS

Exodus 12:1–14
Psalm 116:1–2, 12–19
1 Corinthians 11:23–26
John 13:1–17, 31b–35

CALL TO WORSHIP

Psalm 116:13–14, 17–19

I will lift up the cup of salvation and call on the name of the Lord,
I will pay my vows to the Lord in the presence of all his people.
I will offer to you a thanksgiving sacrifice
and call on the name of the Lord.
I will pay my vows to the Lord in the presence of all his people,
in the courts of the house of the Lord, in your midst, O Jerusalem.
Praise the Lord!

PRAYER OF RENEWAL

Based on John 13:3–5, 14–16

Lord Jesus,
help us to take up the basin and towel,
and minister to those around us.
May we wash the feet of those you bring our way,
seeking not to elevate ourselves in this world,
but following your example to serve others.
We confess that we are often wrapped up in our own lives,
and selfishly seek fortune and fame, comfort and approval.
In those moments, remind us of your humble act, remind us of the gospel,

and bring us to our knees once again, ready to offer our lives in love and service. In the name of Jesus we pray. Amen.

AFFIRMATION OF FAITH

Based on 1 Corinthians 11:23–26

What do we believe concerning the institution of the Lord's Supper?

We believe that the Lord Jesus, on the night when he was betrayed
took a loaf of bread, and when he had given thanks, he broke it and said,
"This is my body that is for you. Do this in remembrance of me."
We believe that in the same way he took the cup also, after supper, saying,
"This cup is the new covenant in my blood. Do this, as often as you drink it,
in remembrance of me."
We believe that as often as we eat the bread and drink the cup,
we proclaim the Lord's death until he comes.

Good Friday (Year A)

LECTIONARY READINGS

Isaiah 52:13–53:12
Psalm 22
Hebrews 4:14–16; 5:7–9
John 18:1–19:42

CALL TO WORSHIP

Psalm 22:1–5

My God, my God, why have you forsaken me?
Why are you so far from helping me, from the words of my groaning?
O my God, I cry by day, but you do not answer; and by night, but find no rest.
Yet you are holy, enthroned on the praises of Israel.
In you our ancestors trusted; they trusted, and you delivered them.
To you they cried, and were saved; in you they trusted, and were not put to shame.

PRAYER OF ADORATION

Based on Isaiah 53:4–6, 10–11

Lord Jesus, we praise you for you bore our infirmities and carried our diseases;
even though we accounted you stricken, struck down by God, and afflicted. You were wounded for our transgressions, crushed for our iniquities;
you suffered the punishment that made us whole, and by your bruises we are healed. We confess that we, like sheep, have gone astray;
we have all turned to our own way, and the Lord has laid on you the iniquity of us all.

Yet, through you the will of the Lord shall prosper; for you are the righteous one,
and you shall make many righteous, and you shall bear our iniquities. Amen.

AFFIRMATION OF FAITH

Based on Hebrews 4:15–16; 5:7–9

What do we believe concerning the high priestly ministry of Christ?

We believe that we do not have a high priest who is unable to sympathize with our weaknesses, but we have one who in every respect has been tested as we are, yet without sin.
We believe, therefore, that we can approach the throne of grace with boldness, so that we may receive mercy and find grace to help in time of need.
We believe that in the days of his flesh, Jesus offered up prayers and supplications, with loud cries and tears, to the one who was able to save him from death, and he was heard because of his reverent submission.
We believe that although he was a Son, he learned obedience through what he suffered; and having been made perfect, he became the source of eternal salvation for all who obey him.

Easter (Year A)

LECTIONARY READINGS

Acts 10:34–43
Psalm 118:1–2, 14–24
Colossians 3:1–4
Matthew 28:1–10

CALL TO WORSHIP

Psalm 118:1, 14

O give thanks to the Lord, for he is good;
his steadfast love endures forever!
The Lord is my strength and my might;
he has become my salvation.

PRAYER OF RENEWAL

Based on Colossians 3:1–4

Risen and ascended Lord,
help us to seek the things that are above,
where you are seated at the right hand of the Father.
By your grace, may we set our minds
on things that are above, not on things that are on earth,
for we have died, and our life is now hidden in you.
You are our life, and when you are revealed,
may we also be revealed with you in glory.
In the name of Jesus we pray. Amen.

AFFIRMATION OF FAITH

Based on Acts 10:38–43

What do we believe about the gospel message?

We believe that God anointed Jesus of Nazareth with the Holy Spirit and with power; that he went about doing good and healing all who were oppressed by the devil, for God was with him.
We believe that he was put to death on a tree;
but God raised him on the third day and allowed him to appear,
not to all the people but to those who were chosen by God as witnesses,
those who ate and drank with him after he rose from the dead.
We believe that he commanded these disciples to preach
and to testify that Jesus is the one ordained by God as judge of the living and the dead.
We believe that all the prophets testify about him and that
everyone who believes in him receives forgiveness of sins through his name.

Second Sunday of Easter (Year A)

LECTIONARY READINGS

Acts 2:14a, 22–32
Psalm 16
1 Peter 1:3–9
John 20:19–31

CALL TO WORSHIP

Psalm 16:7–8, 11

I bless the Lord who gives me counsel;
in the night also my heart instructs me.
I keep the Lord always before me;
because he is at my right hand, I shall not be moved.
**You show me the path of life. In your presence there is fullness of joy;
in your right hand are pleasures forevermore.**

PRAYER OF ADORATION

Based on 1 Peter 1:3–7

Faithful God,
we worship and adore you, for
by your great mercy you have given us a new birth into a living hope
through the resurrection of Jesus Christ from the dead.
You have given us an inheritance that is
imperishable, undefiled, and unfading, kept in heaven for us,
who are being protected by your power through faith
for a salvation ready to be revealed in the last time.
In this we rejoice, even if now for a little while
we have had to suffer various trials, so that
the genuineness of our faith may be found to result

in praise and glory and honor when Jesus Christ is revealed.

AFFIRMATION OF FAITH

Based on Acts 2:22–24

What do we believe regarding God's sovereignty over the death and resurrection of Jesus?

We believe that Jesus of Nazareth, a man attested by God with deeds of power, wonders, and signs that God did through him, was handed over to God's people according to the definite plan and foreknowledge of God.
We believe he was crucified by God's own people
and killed by the hands of those outside the law.
We believe, however, that God raised him up, having freed him from death, because it was impossible for him to be held in its power.

Third Sunday of Easter (Year A)

LECTIONARY READINGS

Acts 2:14a, 36–41
Psalm 116:1–4, 12–19
1 Peter 1:17–23
Luke 24:13–35

CALL TO WORSHIP

Psalm 116:12–14, 17

What shall I return to the Lord for all his bounty to me?
I will lift up the cup of salvation and call on the name of the Lord,
I will pay my vows to the Lord in the presence of all his people.
I will offer to you a thanksgiving sacrifice and call on the name of the Lord.

PRAYER OF RENEWAL

Based on Acts 2:36–38; Luke 24:27, 30–35

Jesus, our Lord and Messiah,
forgive us of our sins and fill us with the Holy Spirit.
Like the disciples on the road to Emmaus,
may we enjoy communion with you
in the breaking of the bread and in the reading of your holy word.
Open our eyes to your work of redemption and grant us
the joy of sharing the good news that the Lord is risen! Amen.

AFFIRMATION OF FAITH

Based on 1 Peter 1:18–19, 21–22

What do we believe concerning the saving blood Christ and genuine mutual love?

We believe that we were ransomed from the futile ways inherited from our ancestors,
not with perishable things like silver or gold, but with the precious blood of Christ, like that of a lamb without defect or blemish.
We believe that we have come to trust in God, who raised Christ from the dead and gave him glory, so that our faith and hope are set on God.
We believe that because we have purified our souls by our obedience to the truth so that we have genuine mutual love, we are to love one another deeply from the heart.

Fourth Sunday of Easter (Good Shepherd Sunday, Year A)

LECTIONARY READINGS

Acts 2:42–47
Psalm 23
1 Peter 2:19–25
John 10:1–10

CALL TO WORSHIP

Psalm 23:1–3

The Lord is my shepherd, I shall not want.
He makes me lie down in green pastures;
he leads me beside still waters; he restores my soul.
He leads me in right paths for his name's sake.

PRAYER OF ADORATION

Based on Psalm 23:1–4; John 10:4, 10

Lord Jesus, we praise you
for you are the Good Shepherd
who leads us beside still waters,
and who restores our souls.
Even when we walk through the darkest valley,
you are there with us to protect and comfort us.
Help us to follow you as you go before us,
and to know your voice as you call us by name.
By your grace, may we have life, and have it abundantly.
In the name of Jesus we pray. Amen.

AFFIRMATION OF FAITH

Based on 1 Peter 2:23–25

What do we believe concerning the way Christ endured pain and suffering?

We believe that when Christ was abused, he did not return abuse; when he suffered, he did not threaten; but he entrusted himself to the one who judges justly.

What do we believe concerning the benefits we have through Christ's suffering?

We believe that Christ bore our sins in his body on the cross, so that, free from sins, we might live for righteousness; by his wounds we have been healed. We believe that we were going astray like sheep, but now, having put our faith in Christ, we have returned to the shepherd and guardian of our souls.

Fifth Sunday of Easter (Year A)

LECTIONARY READINGS

Acts 7:55–60
Psalm 31:1–5, 15–16
1 Peter 2:2–10
John 14:1–14

CALL TO WORSHIP

Psalm 31:1–2

In you, O Lord, I seek refuge;
do not let me ever be put to shame;
in your righteousness deliver me.
Incline your ear to me; rescue me speedily.
Be a rock of refuge for me, a strong fortress to save me.

PRAYER OF RENEWAL

Based on John 14:1–6; Acts 7:55–56

Lord Jesus,
you are the way, the truth, and the light.
Help us to live with the hope
that you are preparing a place for us,
and that where you are, we will be also.
Like Stephen, would you fill us with the Spirit,
that we may we see your glory at the right hand of the Father,
and know your presence with us here on earth.
In the name of Jesus we pray. Amen.

AFFIRMATION OF FAITH

Based on 1 Peter 2:9–10

What do we believe concerning our identity as God's people, the church?

We believe we are a chosen race, a royal priesthood, a holy nation,
God's own people, in order that we may proclaim the mighty acts of him
who called us out of darkness into his marvelous light.
We believe that once we were not a people, but now we are God's people;
once we had not received mercy, but now we have received mercy.

Sixth Sunday of Easter (Year A)

LECTIONARY READINGS

Acts 17:22–31
Psalm 66:8–20
1 Peter 3:13–22
John 14:15–21

CALL TO WORSHIP

Psalm 66:8, 16

Bless our God, O peoples,
let the sound of his praise be heard.
**Come and hear, all you who fear God,
and I will tell what he has done for me.**

PRAYER OF RENEWAL

Based on John 14:15–21

Risen Lord Jesus,
we praise you and thank you
that you have not left us as orphans,
but have given us the promised Holy Spirit,
our Advocate and Comforter;
the one who leads us into righteousness and truth.
We long to keep your commandments,
though we confess we often follow our own way.
By your grace and by your power within us,
help us to love you and live in a manner
that brings honor and glory to your name. Amen.

AFFIRMATION OF FAITH

Based on 1 Peter 3:15–16

What do we believe concerning our testimony for the hope that is within us?

We believe we should always be ready to make our defense to anyone
who demands from us an accounting for the hope that is in us.
We believe, however, that we should offer it with gentleness and reverence.
We believe we should keep our conscience clear, so that, when we are slandered,
those who abuse us for our good conduct in Christ may be put to shame.

Ascension of the Lord (Year A)

LECTIONARY READINGS

Acts 1:1–11
Psalm 47
Ephesians 1:15–23
Luke 24:44–53

CALL TO WORSHIP

Psalm 47:1–2, 5–6

Clap your hands, all you peoples; shout to God with loud songs of joy.
For the Lord, the Most High, is awesome, a great king over all the earth.
**God has gone up with a shout, the Lord with the sound of a trumpet.
Sing praises to God, sing praises; sing praises to our King, sing praises.**

PRAYER OF RENEWAL

Based on Ephesians 1:17–21

Father God, we pray that you would give us
a spirit of wisdom and revelation as we come to know Christ,
so that, with the eyes of our heart enlightened,
we may know the hope to which you have called us,
the riches of Christ's glorious inheritance among the saints,
and the immeasurable greatness of Christ's power for us who believe.
We thank you that you put this power to work in Christ
when you raised him from the dead and seated him
at your right hand in the heavenly places, far above all rule and authority
and power and dominion, and above every name that is named,
not only in this age, but also in the age to come. Amen.

AFFIRMATION OF FAITH

Based on Acts 1:3, 8, 11

What do we believe concerning the earthly appearances and the heavenly ascension of our Lord?

We believe that after he suffered, Jesus presented himself
alive to the apostles by many convincing proofs.
We believe that he appeared to them during forty days and spoke about the kingdom of God.
We believe that, like the apostles, we receive power through the Holy Spirit, and that we, the church, are called to be Christ's witnesses to the ends of the earth.
We believe that Jesus, who was taken up to heaven,
will come again in the same way he departed.

Seventh Sunday of Easter (Year A)

LECTIONARY READINGS

Acts 1:6–14
Psalm 68:1–10, 32–35
1 Peter 4:12–14; 5:6–11
John 17:1–11

CALL TO WORSHIP

Psalm 68:4

Sing to God, sing praises to his name;
lift up a song to him who rides upon the clouds—
his name is the Lord—be exultant before him.

PRAYER OF ADORATION

Based on Acts 1:8–9, 14; John 17:1–11; 1 Peter 4:12–13

Ascended Lord Jesus,
we praise you for you have given us eternal life
and have made yourself known to us.
We ask for your protection,
that we, your people, may be one as you are one.
Help us not to be surprised when we face various trials,
but to rejoice, knowing that we are sharing in your sufferings.
By your grace, may we regularly devote ourselves to prayer,
seeking your strength and power as we live as witnesses
in this world to the grace and glory of the gospel.
In the name of Jesus we pray. Amen.

AFFIRMATION OF FAITH

Based on 1 Peter 5:7–10

What do we believe concerning the comfort and protection of Christ?

We believe that we can cast all our anxiety on him, because he cares for us.
We believe we should discipline ourselves and keep alert, for our adversary, the devil, prowls around like a roaring lion looking for someone to devour.
We believe we are to resist him, remaining steadfast in our faith, for we know that
our brothers and sisters in all the world are undergoing the same kinds of suffering.
We believe that after we have suffered for a little while, the God of all grace, who has called us to his eternal glory in Christ, will himself restore, support, strengthen, and establish us.

Day of Pentecost (Year A)

LECTIONARY READINGS

Acts 2:1–21
Psalm 104:24–34, 35b
1 Corinthians 12:3b–13
John 20:19–23

CALL TO WORSHIP

Psalm 104:33–35

I will sing to the Lord as long as I live;
I will sing praise to my God while I have being.
May my meditation be pleasing to him,
for I rejoice in the Lord.
Bless the Lord, O my soul. Praise the Lord!

PRAYER OF RENEWAL

Based on Acts 2:1–21; John 20:19–23

Lord Jesus,
we thank you for sending the Holy Spirit in power
to your church on the day of Pentecost.
Continue to fill us and renew us in your ways.
Grant us your peace and help us
to experience the Spirit's work in our lives
by not harboring bitterness and resentment,
but by forgiving those who have wronged us and hurt us.
In the name of the Father, Son, and Holy Spirit, we pray. Amen.

AFFIRMATION OF FAITH

Based on 1 Corinthians 12:4–7, 11

What do we believe concerning the gifts of the Spirit?

We believe that there are varieties of gifts, but the same Spirit;
and there are varieties of services, but the same Lord;
and there are varieties of activities, but it is the same God who activates all of them in everyone.
We believe to each is given the manifestation of the Spirit for the common good.
We believe that all of these are activated by one and the same Spirit,
who allots to each one individually just as the Spirit chooses.

Trinity Sunday (Year A)

LECTIONARY READINGS

Genesis 1:1–2:4a
Psalm 8
2 Corinthians 13:11–13
Matthew 28:16–20

CALL TO WORSHIP

Psalm 8:1, 3–5, 9

O Lord, our Sovereign,
how majestic is your name in all the earth!
When I look at your heavens, the work of your fingers,
the moon and the stars that you have established;
what are human beings that you are mindful of them,
mortals that you care for them?
Yet you have made them a little lower than God,
and crowned them with glory and honor.
O Lord, our Sovereign,
how majestic is your name in all the earth!

PRAYER OF RENEWAL

Based on Genesis 1:1–28; Matthew 28:19; 2 Corinthians 13:11–13

Triune God,
we praise you for your work of creation.
We delight in all that you have made
and seek to fulfill the command you have given us
to be fruitful and multiply, to fill the earth and subdue it.
By your grace, may we live in peace with one another,
and carry out the Great Commission to make disciples of all nations.

In all that we do, may the grace of the Lord Jesus Christ,
the love of God, and the communion of the Holy Spirit be with us. Amen.

AFFIRMATION OF FAITH

Based on Matthew 28:18–20

What do we believe concerning the Great Commission?

We believe that Jesus came to the disciples and said to them:
"All authority in heaven and on earth has been given to me. Go therefore and make disciples of all nations, baptizing them in the name of the Father and of the Son and of the Holy Spirit, and teaching them to obey everything that I have commanded you. And remember, I am with you always, to the end of the age."

Proper 3 (Year A)

Sunday between May 24 and May 28 inclusive

LECTIONARY READINGS

Isaiah 49:8–16a
Psalm 131
1 Corinthians 4:1–5
Matthew 6:24–34

CALL TO WORSHIP

Psalm 131

O Lord, my heart is not lifted up, my eyes are not raised too high;
I do not occupy myself with things too great and too marvelous for me.
**But I have calmed and quieted my soul, like a weaned child with its mother;
my soul is like the weaned child that is with me.**
O Israel, hope in the Lord from this time on and forevermore.

PRAYER OF RENEWAL

Based on Matthew 6:25–34

Lord Jesus, our hearts long for rest.
Help us not to worry about our life:
what we will eat or what we will drink,
or about our bodies, what we will wear.
We know that you care for all of your creation,
providing food and nourishment for all living things.
When we become anxious and fearful, by your grace,
help us to trust in your provision for each new day.
May we strive first for your kingdom and your righteousness,
knowing that all of these earthly concerns will be given to us as well.
In the name of Jesus we pray. Amen.

AFFIRMATION OF FAITH

Based on 1 Corinthians 4:1–2

What do we believe concerning the ministry of the apostles?

We believe we are to think of the apostles as servants
of Christ and stewards of God's mysteries.
We believe that it is required of stewards that they be found trustworthy.

Proper 4 (Year A)

Sunday between May 29 and June 4 inclusive

LECTIONARY READINGS

Deuteronomy 11:18–21, 26–28
Psalm 31:1–5, 19–24
Romans 1:16–17; 3:22b–31
Matthew 7:21–29

CALL TO WORSHIP

Psalm 31:1–2, 19

In you, O Lord, I seek refuge; do not let me ever be put to shame;
in your righteousness deliver me. Incline your ear to me; rescue me speedily.
Be a rock of refuge for me, a strong fortress to save me.
O how abundant is your goodness that you have laid up for those who fear you,
and accomplished for those who take refuge in you, in the sight of everyone!

PRAYER OF RENEWAL

Based on Deuteronomy 11:18–21; Matthew 7:24–27

Lord Jesus, help us to put your word in our heart and soul,
feasting on it in such a way that it would nourish us and fill us.
May we be diligent to teach our children about your mighty deeds,
talking about them when we are at home and when we are away,
when we lie down and when we rise.
By your grace, let the truth of the gospel bring abundant blessing upon our lives. Forgive us when we foolishly neglect your word and commandments, finding ourselves vulnerable to temptation; lacking in faith, hope, and love; and quenching our fellowship with the Holy Spirit.

For our desire is to be like a wise man who built his house on rock,
able to withstand the storms and trials of this life, and drawing ever closer
to you. In the name of Jesus we pray. Amen.

AFFIRMATION OF FAITH

Based on Romans 1:16–17; 3:27–28, 30

What do we believe concerning the gospel?

We believe the gospel is the power of God for salvation to everyone who has faith, to the Jew first and also to the Greek. For in it the righteousness of God is revealed through faith for faith; as it is written, "The one who is righteous will live by faith."
We believe there is no room for boasting for we hold that a person is justified by faith apart from works prescribed by the law. God will justify the circumcised on the ground of faith and the uncircumcised through that same faith.

Proper 5 (Year A)

Sunday between June 5 and June 11 inclusive

LECTIONARY READINGS

Hosea 5:15–6:6
Psalm 50:7–15
Romans 4:13–25
Matthew 9:9–13, 18–26

CALL TO WORSHIP

Psalm 50:14–15

Offer to God a sacrifice of thanksgiving,
and pay your vows to the Most High.
Call on me in the day of trouble;
I will deliver you, and you shall glorify me.

PRAYER OF RENEWAL

Based on Matthew 9:12–13; Hosea 6:1, 6

Lord Jesus, help us to understand your words,
"Those who are well have no need of a physician, but those who are sick."
May we see ourselves from your perspective,
and may we be humble and honest about our condition, for we are desperate for you. By your grace, help us not to become self-righteous.
For you desire steadfast love, not sacrifice; genuine fellowship with you, not empty rituals. Let us return to you, O Lord. Amen.

AFFIRMATION OF FAITH

Based on Romans 4:13–14, 16, 23–25

What do we believe concerning the promise given to Abraham?

We believe that the promise that he would inherit the world did not come to Abraham or to his descendants through the law but through the righteousness of faith. If it is the adherents of the law who are to be the heirs, faith is null and the promise is void.
For this reason, we believe the promise depends on faith, in order that it may rest on grace and be guaranteed to all his descendants, not only to the adherents of the law but also to those who share the faith of Abraham.

What do we believe concerning the words, "his faith was reckoned to him as righteousness?"

We believe these words were written not for his sake alone, but for ours also. It will be reckoned to us who believe in him who raised Jesus our Lord from the dead, who was handed over to death for our trespasses and was raised for our justification.

Proper 6 (Year A)

Sunday between June 12 and June 18 inclusive

LECTIONARY READINGS

Exodus 19:2–8a
Psalm 100
Romans 5:1–8
Matthew 9:35–10:23

CALL TO WORSHIP

Psalm 100:1–4

Make a joyful noise to the Lord, all the earth.
Worship the Lord with gladness; come into his presence with singing.
Know that the Lord is God. It is he that made us, and we are his;
we are his people, and the sheep of his pasture.
Enter his gates with thanksgiving, and his courts with praise.
Give thanks to him, bless his name.

PRAYER OF RENEWAL

Based on Matthew 10:5–7, 16, 19–20

Lord Jesus, in the same way that you sent the disciples
to proclaim the good news that the kingdom of heaven has come near;
so empower us and fill us with faith to share this same message with
our neighbors and loved ones who do not yet know you.
As we go, help us to be wise as serpents and innocent as doves.
May we not worry about how we are to speak or what we are to say;
for what we are to say will be given to us at that time;
for it is not we who speak, but the Spirit speaking through us.
In the name of Jesus we pray. Amen.

AFFIRMATION OF FAITH

Based on Romans 5:1, 3–5

What do we believe concerning justification by faith?

We believe that since we are justified by faith,
we have peace with God through our Lord Jesus Christ.

What do we believe concerning suffering?

We believe that suffering produces endurance, and endurance produces character,
and character produces hope, and hope does not disappoint us, because God's love
has been poured into our hearts through the Holy Spirit that has been given to us.

Proper 7 (Year A)

Sunday between June 19 and June 25 inclusive

LECTIONARY READINGS

Jeremiah 20:7–13
Psalm 69:7–18
Romans 6:1b–11
Matthew 10:24–39

CALL TO WORSHIP

Jeremiah 20:13

Sing to the Lord; praise the Lord!
For he has delivered the life of the needy
from the hands of evildoers.

PRAYER OF RENEWAL

Based on Psalm 69:16–18; Matthew 10:30

Answer us, O Lord,
for your steadfast love is good;
according to your abundant mercy, turn to us.
Do not hide your face from your people,
for we are in distress—make haste to answer us.
Draw near to us, redeem us,
set us free from our difficulties.
Because you know us intimately,
help us not to be afraid, but to find rest in you.
In the name of Jesus we pray. Amen.

AFFIRMATION OF FAITH

Based on Romans 6:5–11

What do we believe concerning our union with Christ?

We believe that if we have been united with Christ in a death like his,
we will certainly be united with him in a resurrection like his.
We believe that our old self was crucified with him so that the body of sin might be destroyed
and we might no longer be enslaved to sin. For whoever has died is freed from sin.
But if we have died with Christ, we believe that we will also live with him.
We believe that Christ, being raised from the dead, will never die again;
death no longer has dominion over him. The death he died,
he died to sin, once for all; but the life he lives, he lives to God.
So we also must consider ourselves dead to sin and alive to God in Christ Jesus.

Proper 8 (Year A)

Sunday between June 26 and July 2 inclusive

LECTIONARY READINGS

Jeremiah 28:5–9
Psalm 89:1–4, 15–18
Romans 6:12–23
Matthew 10:40–42

CALL TO WORSHIP

Psalm 89:1–2

I will sing of your steadfast love, O Lord, forever;
with my mouth I will proclaim your faithfulness to all generations.
I declare that your steadfast love is established forever;
your faithfulness is as firm as the heavens.

PRAYER OF RENEWAL

Based on Psalm 89:15–18; Matthew 10:40–42

Sovereign Lord,
we are blessed when we walk
in the light of your countenance.
You are the glory of our strength,
our shield and our protection.
Help us to live lives of generosity and hospitality,
showing kindness to those we encounter,
and offering a cup of cold water to those in need.
In the name of Jesus we pray. Amen.

AFFIRMATION OF FAITH

Based on Romans 6:19, 22–23

What do we believe concerning sin and grace?

We believe that just as we once presented ourselves as slaves
to impurity and to greater and greater iniquity,
so now we present ourselves as slaves to righteousness for sanctification.
We believe that now that we have been freed from sin and enslaved to God,
the advantage we get is sanctification. The end is eternal life.
We believe that the wages of sin is death,
but the free gift of God is eternal life in Christ Jesus our Lord.

Proper 9 (Year A)

Sunday between July 3 and July 9 inclusive

LECTIONARY READINGS

Zechariah 9:9–12
Psalm 145:8–14
Romans 7:15–25a
Matthew 11:16–19, 25–30

CALL TO WORSHIP

Psalm 145:10, 13

All your works shall give thanks to you, O Lord,
and all your faithful shall bless you.
**Your kingdom is an everlasting kingdom,
and your dominion endures throughout all generations.**

PRAYER OF ADORATION

Based on Psalm 145:8–9, 13–14; Matthew 11:28–29

Lord Jesus,
we praise you, for you are gracious and merciful,
slow to anger and abounding in steadfast love.
You are good to all, and your compassion is over all that you have made.
You are faithful in all your words, and gracious in all your deeds.
You uphold all who are falling, and raise up all who are bowed down.
You invite all who are weary and are carrying heavy burdens, to come to you.
For you are gentle and humble in heart, and in you we will find rest for our souls. Amen.

AFFIRMATION OF FAITH

Based on Romans 7:15–25

What do we believe concerning the war between good and evil?

We believe that often we do not do what we want, but we do the very thing we hate.

We believe that that nothing good dwells within us, that is, in our flesh. We can will what is right, but we cannot do it. For we do not do the good we want, but the evil we do not want is what we do. Now if we do what we do not want, it is no longer we that do it, but sin that dwells within us.

We believe that when we want to do what is good, evil lies close at hand. For we delight in the law of God in our inmost selves, but we see in our members another law at war with the law of our minds, making us captive to the law of sin that dwells in our members.

We believe and give thanks to God that, through Jesus Christ our Lord, we are rescued from this body of death.

Proper 10 (Year A)

Sunday between July 10 and July 16 inclusive

LECTIONARY READINGS

Isaiah 55:10–13
Psalm 65
Romans 8:1–11
Matthew 13:1–9, 18–23

CALL TO WORSHIP

Psalm 65:1–2, 4

Praise is due to you, O God, in Zion; and to you shall vows be performed, O you who answer prayer! To you all flesh shall come.
Happy are those whom you choose and bring near to live in your courts.
We shall be satisfied with the goodness of your house, your holy temple.

PRAYER OF RENEWAL

Based on Isaiah 55:10–11; Matthew 13:8

Sovereign God,
we thank you that your word is like the rain
and the snow that come down from heaven,
watering the earth, making it bring forth and sprout,
giving seed to the sower and bread to the eater.
May our hearts be good soil so that as the seed
of your word is sown in us, it would accomplish its purpose,
bearing much fruit in the lives of your people.

AFFIRMATION OF FAITH

Based on Romans 8:1–2, 5–6

What do we believe concerning the Spirit of life in Christ?

We believe that the law of the Spirit of life in Christ Jesus
has set us free from the law of sin and of death.
We believe that those who live according to the flesh
set their minds on the things of the flesh,
but those who live according to the Spirit
set their minds on the things of the Spirit.
We believe that to set the mind on the flesh is death,
but to set the mind on the Spirit is life and peace.

Proper 11 (Year A)

Sunday between July 17 and July 23 inclusive

LECTIONARY READINGS

Isaiah 44:6–8
Psalm 86:11–17
Romans 8:12–25
Matthew 13:24–30, 36–43

CALL TO WORSHIP

Psalm 86:11–12

Teach me your way, O Lord, that I may walk in your truth;
give me an undivided heart to revere your name.
**I give thanks to you, O Lord my God,
with my whole heart, and I will glorify your name forever.**

PRAYER OF RENEWAL

Based on Psalm 86:11; Romans 8:14–17, 24–25; Matthew 13:37–38

Holy God, teach us your way,
that we may walk in your truth;
give us undivided hearts to revere your name.
Remind us that we have been adopted by you;
that your Spirit bears witness with our spirit that we are your children.
Help us to place our hope in what we do not see
and rest in knowing that we are children of the kingdom,
the good seed that you have sown.
In the name of Jesus we pray. Amen.

AFFIRMATION OF FAITH

Based on Romans 8:14–17

What do we believe concerning our adoption as children of God?

We believe that we who are led by the Spirit of God
are children of God. For we did not receive a spirit of slavery
to fall back into fear, but we have received a spirit of adoption.
We believe that when we cry, "Abba! Father!" it is that very Spirit
bearing witness with our spirit that we are children of God,
and if children, then heirs, heirs of God and joint heirs with Christ—
if, in fact, we suffer with him so that we may also be glorified with him.

Proper 12 (Year A)

Sunday between July 24 and July 30 inclusive

LECTIONARY READINGS

1 Kings 3:5–12
Psalm 119:129–136
Romans 8:26–39
Matthew 13:31–33, 44–52

CALL TO WORSHIP

Psalm 119:129–131

Your decrees are wonderful; therefore my soul keeps them.
The unfolding of your words gives light;
it imparts understanding to the simple.
With open mouth I pant, because I long for your commandments.

PRAYER OF RENEWAL

Based on Psalm 119:132–33; 1 Kings 3:9; Romans 8:26–27;
Matthew 13:31–33, 44–46

Holy God, turn to us and be gracious to us.
Keep our steps steady according to your promise,
and never let iniquity have dominion over us.
Give us understanding minds and help us to discern between good and evil.
May your Spirit intercede for us with sighs too deep for words.
Fill us with the joy and power of the kingdom,
making disciples of all nations and finding our greatest treasure in you.
In the name of Jesus we pray. Amen.

AFFIRMATION OF FAITH

Based on Romans 8:26–30

What do we believe concerning the Spirit and prayer?

We believe the Spirit helps us in our weakness; for we do not know how to pray as we ought,
but that very Spirit intercedes with sighs too deep for words.
We believe the Spirit intercedes for the saints according to the will of God.

What do we believe concerning predestination?

We believe that all things work together for good for those who love God, who are called according to his purpose. For those whom he foreknew he also predestined to be conformed to the image of his Son, in order that Jesus might be the firstborn within a large family.
We believe that those whom he predestined he also called; and those whom he called he also justified; and those whom he justified he also glorified.

Proper 13 (Year A)

Sunday between July 31 and August 6 inclusive

LECTIONARY READINGS

Isaiah 55:1–5
Psalm 145:8–9, 14–21
Romans 9:1–5
Matthew 14:13–21

CALL TO WORSHIP

Isaiah 55:1–2

Come, everyone who thirsts, come to the waters; and you that have no money, come, buy and eat! Come, buy wine and milk without money and without price.
**Why do you spend your money for that which is not bread,
and your labor for that which does not satisfy?
Listen carefully to me, and eat what is good, and delight yourselves in rich food.**

PRAYER OF ADORATION

Based on Isaiah 55:1–2; Psalm 145:8–9, 15–16; Matthew 14:13–21

Lord Jesus,
we praise you for the abundance of your grace and mercy,
for you are slow to anger and abounding in steadfast love.
You invite us to feast freely on all that you provide,
for you are good to all, and your compassion is over all that you have made.
The eyes of all look to you, and you give us our food in due season.
You open your hand, satisfying the desire of every living thing.
As you fed the multitudes long ago with only five loaves and two fish,

so satisfy the hunger in our souls today with the nourishment of your word and Spirit.
In the name of Jesus we pray. Amen.

AFFIRMATION OF FAITH

Based on Psalm 145:8–9, 14, 17–18

What do we believe concerning the character of God?

We believe the Lord is gracious and merciful, slow to anger and abounding in steadfast love.
We believe the Lord is good to all, and his compassion is over all that he has made.
We believe the Lord upholds all who are falling, and raises up all who are bowed down.
We believe the Lord is just in all his ways, and kind in all his doings.
We believe the Lord is near to all who call on him, to all who call on him in truth.

Proper 14 (Year A)

Sunday between August 7 and August 13 inclusive

LECTIONARY READINGS

1 Kings 19:9–18
Psalm 85:8–13
Romans 10:5–15
Matthew 14:22–33

CALL TO WORSHIP

Psalm 85:8

Let me hear what God the Lord will speak,
for he will speak peace to his people,
to his faithful, to those who turn to him in their hearts.
Surely his salvation is at hand for those who fear him,
that his glory may dwell in our land.

PRAYER OF RENEWAL

Based on 1 Kings 19:9–18; Matthew 14:22–33

Lord Jesus,
we know you are powerful, able to stir up
great winds, earthquakes, and fires.
Yet, you often choose to speak to us, as you spoke to Elijah,
through silence and with a still, small voice.
Like the disciples, may we see your power
to calm the storms in our lives.
Help us to put our faith in you and worship you in all circumstances;
knowing deeply and trusting wholly that you are the Son of God.
In the name of Jesus we pray. Amen.

AFFIRMATION OF FAITH

Based on Romans 10:9, 12

What do we believe concerning salvation?

We believe that if you confess with your lips that Jesus is Lord
and believe in your heart that God raised him from the dead, you will be saved.

Do we believe salvation is for all people, Jews and gentiles alike?

Yes. We believe there is no distinction between Jew and gentile;
the same Lord is Lord of all and is generous to all who call on him.
For "Everyone who calls on the name of the Lord shall be saved."

Proper 15 (Year A)

Sunday between August 14 and August 20 inclusive

LECTIONARY READINGS

Isaiah 56:1, 6–8
Psalm 67
Romans 11:1–2a, 29–32
Matthew 15:10–28

CALL TO WORSHIP

Psalm 67:4–5

Let the nations be glad and sing for joy,
for you judge the peoples with equity and guide the nations upon earth.
Let the peoples praise you, O God; let all the peoples praise you.

PRAYER OF RENEWAL

Based on Psalm 67:1–3; Isaiah 56:6–7; Matthew 15:10–20

Lord Jesus,
we know that one day all the nations of the earth will praise you,
people from every tribe and tongue will bow before your throne.
Help us to be a light to those around us,
declaring your mighty deeds and saving power;
for you desire that your house would be a house of prayer for all peoples.
And by your grace, would you cleanse our hearts,
so that the words of our mouth would not
slander, curse, or ridicule, but edify, encourage,
and bless you, our neighbors, our family members, and friends.
In the name of Jesus we pray. Amen.

AFFIRMATION OF FAITH

Based on Matthew 15:11, 18–19

What do we believe concerning the words that come out of our mouth and the nature of our heart?

We believe that it is not what goes into the mouth
that defiles a person, but it is what comes out of the mouth that defiles.
We believe that what comes out of the mouth
proceeds from the heart, and this is what defiles.
We believe that out of the heart come evil intentions,
murder, adultery, fornication, theft, false witness, slander.

Proper 16 (Year A)

Sunday between August 21 and August 27 inclusive

LECTIONARY READINGS

Isaiah 51:1–6
Psalm 138
Romans 12:1–8
Matthew 16:13–20

CALL TO WORSHIP

Psalm 138:1–2

I give you thanks, O Lord, with my whole heart;
before the gods I sing your praise;
**I bow down toward your holy temple and give thanks to your name
for your steadfast love and your faithfulness;
for you have exalted your name and your word above everything.**

PRAYER OF RENEWAL

Based on Matthew 16:16; Isaiah 51:1–6

Lord Jesus,
we believe that you are the Messiah, the Son of the living God.
Help us to pursue your righteousness
and to seek you in all things.
Thank you for the many ways you comfort us,
and bring refreshment to the parched places of our lives.
May your people be full of joy and gladness;
may songs of thanksgiving be on our lips.
Encourage us to be messengers of the good news
of your salvation to all the nations of the earth.
Your salvation is forever, and your deliverance will never end.

In the name of Jesus we pray. Amen.

AFFIRMATION OF FAITH

Based on Romans 12:1–2

What do we believe concerning our spiritual act of worship?

We believe that, by the mercies of God, we are to present our bodies as living sacrifices, holy and acceptable to God, which is our spiritual worship.

What do we believe concerning the renewing of our minds?

We believe that we are not to be conformed to this world,
but to be transformed by the renewing of our minds,
so that we may discern what is the will of God—what is good and acceptable and perfect.

Proper 17 (Year A)

Sunday between August 28 and September 3 inclusive

LECTIONARY READINGS

Jeremiah 15:15–21
Psalm 26:1–8
Romans 12:9–21
Matthew 16:21–28

CALL TO WORSHIP

Psalm 26:1–3, 8

Vindicate me, O Lord, for I have walked in my integrity, and I have trusted in the Lord without wavering. Prove me, O Lord, and try me; test my heart and mind.
For your steadfast love is before my eyes, and I walk in faithfulness to you. O Lord, I love the house in which you dwell, and the place where your glory abides.

PRAYER OF RENEWAL

Based on Matthew 16:24–26; Psalm 26:1, 3

Lord Jesus,
we know that if we want to become your followers,
we must deny ourselves, take up our cross, and follow you.
If we truly desire to save our life, we will lose it;
and if we lose our life for your sake, we will find it.
By your grace, may we see the foolishness in striving
to gain the whole world while forfeiting our soul.
Help us to walk in integrity and trust you without wavering.
May your steadfast love be before our eyes as we seek to walk in faithfulness to you. In the name of Jesus we pray. Amen.

AFFIRMATION OF FAITH

Based on Romans 12:9–10, 12–15

What do we believe concerning how are we to live together as followers of Christ?

We believe we are to let love be genuine; hate what is evil, hold fast to what is good;
love one another with mutual affection; and outdo one another in showing honor.
We believe we are to rejoice in hope, be patient in suffering, persevere in prayer;
contribute to the needs of the saints; and extend hospitality to strangers.
We believe we are to bless those who persecute us;
rejoice with those who rejoice, and weep with those who weep.

Proper 18 (Year A)

Sunday between September 4 and September 10 inclusive

LECTIONARY READINGS

Ezekiel 33:7–11
Psalm 119:33–40
Romans 13:8–14
Matthew 18:15–20

CALL TO WORSHIP

Psalm 119:33–35

Teach me, O Lord, the way of your statutes, and I will observe it to the end.
Give me understanding, that I may keep your law and observe it with my whole heart.
Lead me in the path of your commandments, for I delight in it.

PRAYER OF RENEWAL

Based on Matthew 18:15–20

Gracious God,
help us to live at peace with one another.
When we sin against someone,
help us to promptly ask for forgiveness;
and when we are sinned against, give us the courage
to go to our offender and seek reconciliation.
May we fulfill your commandments by loving you
with all of our heart, soul, mind, and strength,
and by loving our neighbor as ourselves.
In the name of Jesus we pray. Amen.

AFFIRMATION OF FAITH

Based on Romans 13:8–10

What do we believe concerning the law and our love for one another?

We believe we are not to owe anyone anything, except to love one another; for the one who loves another has fulfilled the law.
We believe that the commandments, "You shall not commit adultery; You shall not murder;
You shall not steal; You shall not covet"; and any other commandment, are summed up in this word, "Love your neighbor as yourself."
We believe that love does no wrong to a neighbor; therefore, love is the fulfilling of the law.

Proper 19 (Year A)

Sunday between September 11 and September 17 inclusive

LECTIONARY READINGS

Genesis 50:15–21
Psalm 103:1–13
Romans 14:1–12
Matthew 18:21–35

CALL TO WORSHIP

Psalm 103:1–5

Bless the Lord, O my soul, and all that is within me, bless his holy name. **Bless the Lord, O my soul, and do not forget all his benefits—who forgives all your iniquity, who heals all your diseases, who redeems your life from the Pit, who crowns you with steadfast love and mercy, who satisfies you with good as long as you live so that your youth is renewed like the eagle's.**

PRAYER OF RENEWAL

Based on Matthew 18:21–35; Genesis 50:19–20

Sovereign God,
help us to extend the same mercy and forgiveness
to others that you have given to us.
By your grace, may we not forget the kindness
we have been shown, but offer that same love
to our neighbors, our family members, and friends.
Even when others do us harm, remind us of your sovereign care,
for we know you are able to redeem our trials for our good and your glory.
In the name of Jesus we pray. Amen.

AFFIRMATION OF FAITH

Based on Romans 14:7–10

How are we to live and love one another without judgment?

We believe that we do not live to ourselves, and we do not die to ourselves.
If we live, we live to the Lord, and if we die, we die to the Lord;
so then, whether we live or whether we die, we are the Lord's.
For to this end Christ died and lived again,
so that he might be Lord of both the dead and the living.
We believe that we are not to pass judgment on our brother or our sister.
We are not to despise our brother or our sister,
for we will all stand before the judgment seat of God.

Proper 20 (Year A)

Sunday between September 18 and September 24 inclusive

LECTIONARY READINGS

Jonah 3:10–4:11
Psalm 145:1–8
Philippians 1:21–30
Matthew 20:1–16

CALL TO WORSHIP

Psalm 145:1–3

I will extol you, my God and King,
and bless your name forever and ever.
Every day I will bless you,
and praise your name forever and ever.
Great is the Lord, and greatly to be praised;
his greatness is unsearchable.

PRAYER OF RENEWAL

Based on Jonah 4:2; Matthew 20:1–16

Sovereign Lord,
you are gracious and merciful,
slow to anger and abounding in steadfast love.
You do not treat us as we deserve,
but offer us grace and love despite our selfish ways.
Help us to bring your kingdom where we live and work,
demonstrating your love and mercy to others;
and extending grace and forgiveness to
our neighbors, our family, our friends, and even our enemies.
In the name of Jesus we pray. Amen.

AFFIRMATION OF FAITH

Based on Philippians 1:27–28

How are we to live as godly examples in this world?

We believe we are to live our lives
in a manner worthy of the gospel of Christ,
standing firm in one spirit, striving side by side
with one mind for the faith of the gospel;
being in no way intimidated by our opponents.

Proper 21 (Year A)

Sunday between September 25 and October 1 inclusive

LECTIONARY READINGS

Ezekiel 18:1–4, 25–32
Psalm 25:1–9
Philippians 2:1–13
Matthew 21:23–32

CALL TO WORSHIP

Psalm 25:1, 4–5

To you, O Lord, I lift up my soul.
Make me to know your ways, O Lord; teach me your paths.
Lead me in your truth, and teach me,
for you are the God of my salvation; for you I wait all day long.

PRAYER OF RENEWAL

Based on Matthew 21:23–32; Philippians 2:3–5

Lord Jesus,
help us to never question your authority,
but humbly submit to your sovereign care over our lives.
By your grace, may we do nothing from selfish ambition or conceit,
but, in humility, regard others as better than ourselves.
May we not look to your own interests, but to the interests of others.
Give us your mind, your heart, your desires.
In the name of Jesus we pray. Amen.

AFFIRMATION OF FAITH

Based on Philippians 2:6–11

What do we believe concerning the humiliation and the exaltation of Christ?

We believe that Christ, though he was in the form of God,
did not regard equality with God as something to be exploited,
but emptied himself, taking the form of a slave, being born in human likeness.
We believe that, being found in human form, he humbled himself
and became obedient to the point of death—even death on a cross.
We believe, therefore, that God also highly exalted him and gave him the name that is above every name,
so that at the name of Jesus every knee should bend,
in heaven and on earth and under the earth, and every tongue should confess that Jesus Christ is Lord, to the glory of God the Father.

Proper 22 (Year A)

Sunday between October 2 and October 8 inclusive

LECTIONARY READINGS

Isaiah 5:1–7
Psalm 80:7–15
Philippians 3:4b–14
Matthew 21:33–46

CALL TO WORSHIP

Matthew 21:42

The stone that the builders rejected has become the cornerstone;
this was the Lord's doing, and it is amazing in our eyes.

PRAYER OF RENEWAL

Based on Matthew 21:33–46; Philippians 3:8

Lord Jesus,
we are like a vineyard which you have planted;
help us, by your grace, to produce kingdom fruit
through lives wholly devoted to you.
May we regard everything as loss compared
to the surpassing value of knowing you as our Lord.
You are the cornerstone, our solid foundation.
Use us for your purposes.
In the name of Jesus we pray. Amen.

AFFIRMATION OF FAITH

Based on Philippians 3:7–9

What do we believe concerning our earthly accomplishments?

We believe we are to regard everything as loss
because of the surpassing value of knowing Christ Jesus our Lord.
We believe that for his sake we have suffered the loss of all things,
and we regard them as rubbish, in order that we may gain Christ and be found in him,
not having a righteousness of our own that comes from the law,
but one that comes through faith in Christ, the righteousness from God based on faith.

Proper 23 (Year A)

Sunday between October 9 and October 15 inclusive

LECTIONARY READINGS

Isaiah 25:1–9
Psalm 23
Philippians 4:1–9
Matthew 22:1–14

CALL TO WORSHIP

Isaiah 25:1

O Lord, you are my God;
I will exalt you, I will praise your name;
for you have done wonderful things,
plans formed of old, faithful and sure.

PRAYER OF RENEWAL

Based on Matthew 22:1–10; Psalm 23:2–4; Philippians 4:8–9

Sovereign God,
you are the Good Shepherd who leads us beside still waters,
inviting us to feast on your gospel promises.
Yet, too often we make light of them and live our lives the way we desire.
May we see the mercy you grant us:
when we are weary, you restore our souls;
when we walk through difficult trials,
you carry us and make your presence known to us.
Oh Lord, forgive us and fill us with your Holy Spirit.
Seeking your peace, may we dwell on what is true, honorable,
just, pure, pleasing, commendable, excellent, and praiseworthy.
In the name of Jesus we pray. Amen.

AFFIRMATION OF FAITH

Based on Philippians 4:4–7

What do we believe concerning how we are to live by faith in anxious times?

We believe we are to rejoice in the Lord always.
We believe we are to let our gentleness be known to everyone.
We believe the Lord is near; therefore, we do not worry about anything,
but in everything by prayer and supplication with thanksgiving
we let our requests be made known to God.
In all of this, we believe the peace of God, which surpasses all understanding,
will guard our hearts and our minds in Christ Jesus.

Proper 24 (Year A)

Sunday between October 16 and October 22 inclusive

LECTIONARY READINGS

Isaiah 45:1–7
Psalm 96:1–13
1 Thessalonians 1:1–10
Matthew 22:15–22

CALL TO WORSHIP

Psalm 96:1–4

O sing to the Lord a new song;
sing to the Lord, all the earth.
Sing to the Lord, bless his name;
tell of his salvation from day to day.
Declare his glory among the nations,
his marvelous works among all the peoples.
For great is the Lord, and greatly to be praised;
he is to be revered above all gods.

PRAYER OF RENEWAL

Based on Isaiah 45:2; Psalm 96:7–8; 1 Thessalonians 1:3, 8

Lord Jesus,
we know that you go before us and clear our path.
May we ascribe to you all the glory that is due your name.
Like the Thessalonians, may the world see our work of faith,
our labor of love, and our steadfastness of hope in the Lord Jesus Christ.
May the good news of the gospel sound forth from us in our city,
and in every place that our faith in God has become known.
In the name of Jesus we pray. Amen.

AFFIRMATION OF FAITH

Based on Matthew 22:21

What do we believe concerning our responsibilities to our country and to the Lord?

We believe we are to give to our government
the things that are our government's, and to God the things that are God's.

Proper 25 (Year A)

Sunday between October 23 and October 29 inclusive

LECTIONARY READINGS

Leviticus 19:1–2, 15–18
Psalm 1
1 Thessalonians 2:1–8
Matthew 22:34–46

CALL TO WORSHIP

Psalm 1:1–2

Happy are those who do not follow the advice of the wicked,
or take the path that sinners tread, or sit in the seat of scoffers;
but their delight is in the law of the Lord,
and on his law they meditate day and night.

PRAYER OF RENEWAL

Based on Psalm 1:2–3; Matthew 22:37–39

Gracious God,
help us to be like trees planted by streams of living water,
bearing fruit for your kingdom.
May we take delight in all of your commands:
loving you with all of our heart, all of our soul,
and all of our mind; and loving our neighbors as ourselves.
In the name of Jesus we pray. Amen.

AFFIRMATION OF FAITH

Based on Matthew 22:37–40

What do we believe are the two greatest commandments?

We believe that Jesus said the two greatest commandments are
to love the Lord your God with all your heart, and with all your soul,
and with all your mind; and to love your neighbor as yourself.
We believe Jesus said, "On these two commandments hang all the law and
the prophets."

Proper 26 (Year A)

Sunday between October 30 and November 5 inclusive

LECTIONARY READINGS

Micah 3:5–12
Psalm 43
1 Thessalonians 2:9–13
Matthew 23:1–12

CALL TO WORSHIP

Psalm 43:3–4

O send out your light and your truth; let them lead me;
let them bring me to your holy hill and to your dwelling.
**Then I will go to the altar of God, to God my exceeding joy;
and I will praise you with the harp, O God, my God.**

PRAYER OF RENEWAL

Based on Matthew 23:1–12

Triune God,
help us to remember that all who exalt themselves will be humbled,
and all who humble themselves will be exalted.
May we not be like those who want all of their deeds to be seen by others;
who seek to have the place of honor at banquets and gatherings;
who tie up heavy burdens, hard to bear, and lay them on the shoulders of
others. By your grace, may we practice what we preach,
pursuing justice and mercy, not outward appearances.
Give us the desire to love and care for others
through the power of your Holy Spirit at work within us.
In the name of Jesus we pray. Amen.

AFFIRMATION OF FAITH

Based on 1 Thessalonians 2:13

How are we to receive the word of God?

We believe we are to accept it not as a human word,
but as what it really is, God's word.
We believe this word is at work in us who follow Christ.

Proper 27 (Year A)

Sunday between November 6 and November 12 inclusive

LECTIONARY READINGS

Amos 5:18–24
Psalm 70
1 Thessalonians 4:13–18
Matthew 25:1–13

CALL TO WORSHIP

Psalm 70:4

Let all who seek you rejoice and be glad in you.
Let those who love your salvation say evermore, "God is great!"

PRAYER OF RENEWAL

Based on Matthew 25:1–13; Amos 5:18–24

Lord Jesus,
may we be ready for your return.
Help us to live in anticipation of the fullness of your kingdom.
In your church and world, let justice roll down like waters,
and righteousness like an ever-flowing stream;
and may we be instruments of this kind of love and mercy.
May our expressions of worship not be in vain,
but a reflection of hearts and lives fully devoted to you.
In the name of Jesus we pray. Amen.

AFFIRMATION OF FAITH

Based on 1 Thessalonians 4:16–17

What do we believe concerning Christ's return?

We believe that the Lord himself, with a cry of command,
with the archangel's call and with the sound of God's trumpet,
will descend from heaven, and the dead in Christ will rise first.
Then we who are alive, who are left,
will be caught up in the clouds together with them
to meet the Lord in the air; and so we will be with the Lord forever.

Proper 28 (Year A)

Sunday between November 13 and November 19 inclusive

LECTIONARY READINGS

Zephaniah 1:7, 12–18
Psalm 90:1–12
1 Thessalonians 5:1–11
Matthew 25:14–30

CALL TO WORSHIP

Psalm 90:1–2

Lord, you have been our dwelling place
in all generations.
**Before the mountains were brought forth,
or ever you had formed the earth and the world,
from everlasting to everlasting you are God.**

PRAYER OF RENEWAL

Based on Psalm 90:1, 12; Matthew 25:14–30

Faithful God,
you have been our dwelling place in all generations.
Teach us to count our days that we may gain a wise heart.
Help us to steward the gifts and talents you have given us
for the expansion of your kingdom; for we know that to all those who have,
more will be given, and they will have an abundance.
As we anticipate the day of your return, may we live generous
and sober lives before you and others. In the name of Jesus we pray. Amen.

AFFIRMATION OF FAITH

Based on 1 Thessalonians 5:2, 8–10

What do we believe concerning the day of the Lord?

We believe that the day of the Lord will come like a thief in the night.

How are we to live in light of the coming day of the Lord?

We believe we are to be sober and put on the breastplate of faith and love, and for a helmet the hope of salvation. For God has destined us not for wrath but for obtaining salvation through our Lord Jesus Christ, who died for us, so that whether we are awake or asleep we may live with him.

Christ the King (Year A)

LECTIONARY READINGS

Ezekiel 34:11–16, 20–24
Psalm 95:1–7a
Ephesians 1:15–23
Matthew 25:31–46

CALL TO WORSHIP

Psalm 95:1–2

O come, let us sing to the Lord;
let us make a joyful noise to the rock of our salvation!
Let us come into his presence with thanksgiving;
let us make a joyful noise to him with songs of praise!

PRAYER OF RENEWAL

Based on Matthew 25:31–40

Christ our King,
we know that on the day that you come in your glory,
you will gather all the nations and separate people,
one from another, as a shepherd separates the sheep from the goats.
May we be counted among the sheep,
the righteous ones who demonstrated your love to others:
giving food to the hungry; offering drink to the thirsty;
welcoming the stranger;
clothing the naked; taking care of the sick; and visiting those in prison.
For what is done unto the least of these,
your brothers and sisters, is done unto you.
In the name of Jesus we pray. Amen.

AFFIRMATION OF FAITH

Based on Ephesians 1:20–23

What do we believe concerning God's power at work in Christ?

We believe that God put his power to work in Christ
when he raised him from the dead and seated him at his right hand in the heavenly places,
far above all rule and authority and power and dominion,
and above every name that is named, not only in this age but also in the age to come.
We believe God has put all things under Jesus' feet and has made him the head over all things for the church,
which is his body, the fullness of him who fills all in all.

The Year of Mark

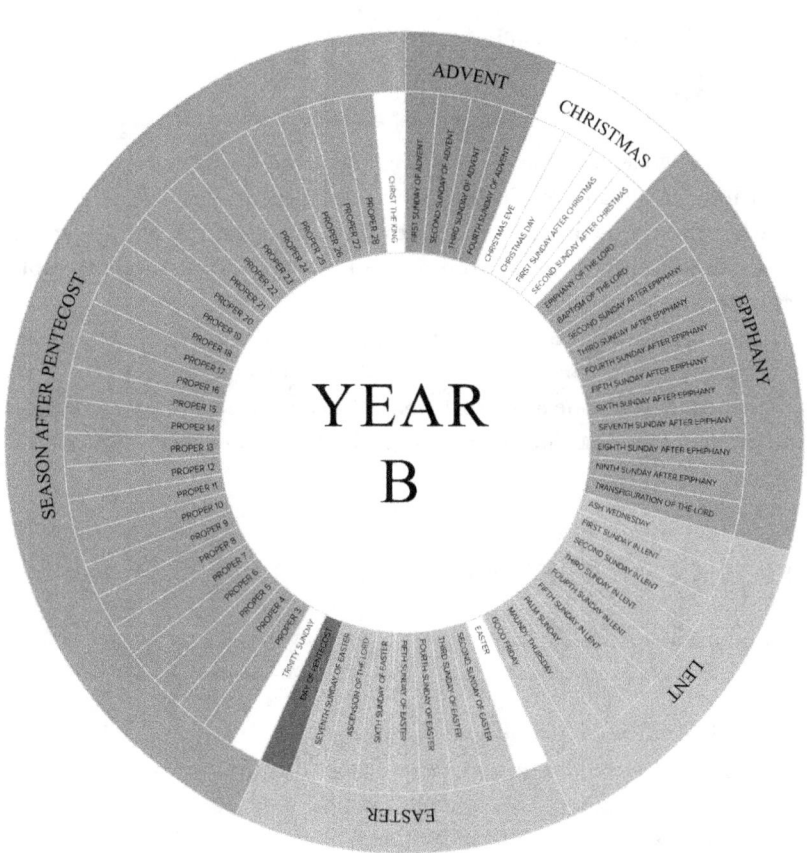

First Sunday of Advent (Year B)

LECTIONARY READINGS

Isaiah 64:1–9
Psalm 80:1–7, 17–19
1 Corinthians 1:3–9
Mark 13:24–37

CALL TO WORSHIP

Isaiah 64:1–4

O that you would tear open the heavens and come down,
so that the mountains would quake at your presence—
as when fire kindles brushwood and the fire causes water to boil—to make your name known to your adversaries, so that the nations might tremble at your presence!
When you did awesome deeds that we did not expect,
you came down, the mountains quaked at your presence.
From ages past no one has heard, no ear has perceived,
no eye has seen any God besides you, who works for those who wait for him.

PRAYER OF RENEWAL

Based on Mark 13:28–37

Lord Jesus,
no one knows the day or the hour of your return.
During this Advent season, may we be alert and awake,
watchful for the signs of your second coming.
As we understand the coming of summer,
so, too, may we understand when the day of the Lord is drawing near.
Until that time, set our hearts on you and your kingdom

and help us to live in the hope that all will be made new.
In the name of Jesus we pray. Amen.

AFFIRMATION OF FAITH

Based on 1 Corinthians 1:5–8

How are we equipped for Christ's second coming?

We believe that we have been enriched in Christ in every way,
in speech and knowledge of every kind so that we are not lacking
in any spiritual gift as we wait for the revealing of our Lord Jesus Christ.
We believe he will also strengthen us to the end,
so that we may be blameless on the day of our Lord Jesus Christ.

Second Sunday of Advent (Year B)

LECTIONARY READINGS

Isaiah 40:1–11
Psalm 85:1–2, 8–13
2 Peter 3:8–15a
Mark 1:1–8

CALL TO WORSHIP

Psalm 85:8–9

Let me hear what God the Lord will speak,
for he will speak peace to his people,
to his faithful, to those who turn to him in their hearts.
Surely his salvation is at hand for those who fear him,
that his glory may dwell in our land.

PRAYER OF RENEWAL

Based on Mark 1:2–3; 2 Peter 3:14–15

Lord Jesus,
during this Advent season,
we think of John the Baptist, the one who came before you,
to prepare your way through the confession of sin and baptism.
May your indwelling Spirit speak into our hearts today
and lead us to repentance, that we may strive
to be found by you without spot or blemish, and at peace;
and may we regard your patience as salvation.
In the name of Jesus we pray. Amen.

AFFIRMATION OF FAITH

Based on 2 Peter 3:8–9, 13–15

What do we believe concerning the coming of the Lord?

We believe that with the Lord one day is like a thousand years,
and a thousand years are like one day.
We believe the Lord is not slow about his promise, as some think of slowness,
but is patient with us, not wanting any to perish, but all to come to repentance.

How are we to live until the Lord returns?

In accordance with his promise, we wait for new heavens and a new earth,
where righteousness is at home. While we are waiting for these things,
we strive to be found by him at peace, without spot or blemish;
and we regard the patience of our Lord as salvation.

Third Sunday of Advent (Year B)

LECTIONARY READINGS

Isaiah 61:1–4, 8–11
Psalm 126
1 Thessalonians 5:16–24
John 1:6–8, 19–28

CALL TO WORSHIP

Isaiah 61:11

For as the earth brings forth its shoots,
and as a garden causes what is sown in it to spring up,
so the Lord God will cause righteousness and praise
to spring up before all the nations.

PRAYER OF RENEWAL

Based on Isaiah 61:1; 1 Thessalonians 5:16–23

Lord Jesus,
during this Advent season,
we recognize you as the Messiah, the anointed one sent
to bring good news to the oppressed, to bind up the brokenhearted,
to proclaim liberty to the captives, and release to the prisoners.
Help us, O Lord, to rejoice always, to pray without ceasing,
and to give thanks in all circumstances; for this is your will for us.
May we not quench the Spirit, but hold fast to what is good;
and abstain from every form of evil.
Our desire is for you to sanctify us entirely;
and for our spirit and soul and body to be kept sound and blameless at your
return. In the name of Jesus we pray. Amen.

AFFIRMATION OF FAITH

Based on John 1:6–8, 19–23

What do we believe concerning the ministry of John the Baptist?

We believe he was a man sent from God, whose name was John.
We believe he came as a witness to testify to the light,
so that all might believe through him.
He himself was not the light, but he came to testify to the light.

Was he the Messiah, Elijah, or the prophet?

No. We believe that he was the voice of one crying out in the wilderness,
"Make straight the way of the Lord," as the prophet Isaiah said.

Fourth Sunday of Advent (Year B)

LECTIONARY READINGS

2 Samuel 7:1–11, 16
Psalm 89:1–4, 19–26
Romans 16:25–27
Luke 1:26–38

CALL TO WORSHIP

Psalm 89:1–2

I will sing of your steadfast love, O Lord, forever;
with my mouth I will proclaim your faithfulness to all generations.
**I declare that your steadfast love is established forever;
your faithfulness is as firm as the heavens.**

PRAYER OF RENEWAL

Based on Luke 1:29, 31; Romans 16:25–26; 2 Samuel 7:16

Lord Jesus, like Mary, we are often perplexed
and ponder the mystery of your birth.
How could it be that the God of the universe
took on flesh and dwelt among us?
How could it be that a virgin was pregnant
with a child conceived by the Holy Spirit?
O Lord, may we be strengthened by the gospel
and the proclamation of Jesus Christ,
according to the revelation of the mystery
that was kept secret for long ages but is now disclosed.
Help us to share this good news with family, friends, and neighbors;
and may you receive all glory and praise, for your throne
and your kingdom are established forever. Amen.

AFFIRMATION OF FAITH

Based on Luke 1:26–27, 30–33

What do we believe concerning the foretelling of Jesus' birth?

We believe the angel Gabriel was sent by God to a town in Galilee called Nazareth,
to a virgin engaged to a man whose name was Joseph, of the house of David. The virgin's name was Mary.
We believe the angel said to her, "Do not be afraid, Mary, for you have found favor with God. And now, you will conceive in your womb and bear a son, and you will name him Jesus. He will be great, and will be called the Son of the Most High, and the Lord God will give to him the throne of his ancestor David. He will reign over the house of Jacob forever, and of his kingdom there will be no end."

Christmas Eve (Year B)

LECTIONARY READINGS

Isaiah 9:2–7
Psalm 96
Titus 2:11–14
Luke 2:1–20

CALL TO WORSHIP

Psalm 96:1–3

O sing to the Lord a new song; sing to the Lord, all the earth.
Sing to the Lord, bless his name; tell of his salvation from day to day.
Declare his glory among the nations, his marvelous works among all the peoples.

PRAYER OF ADORATION

Based on Isaiah 9:2–7

Blessed Savior, we worship you, for you are the light
that shines in the darkness.
You are the Son who has been given to us;
authority rests upon your shoulders; and you are named
Wonderful Counselor, Mighty God,
Everlasting Father, Prince of Peace.
We praise you, for you will establish and uphold your kingdom
with justice and with righteousness forever.
In the name of Jesus we pray. Amen.

AFFIRMATION OF FAITH

Based on Luke 2:1–14

What do we believe concerning the story of Jesus' birth?

We believe that Joseph went from the town of Nazareth in Galilee to Judea, to the city of David called Bethlehem, because he was descended from the house and family of David. He went to be registered with Mary, to whom he was engaged and who was expecting a child. While they were there, she gave birth to Jesus, her firstborn son. She wrapped him in bands of cloth, and laid him in a manger, because there was no place for them in the inn.

We believe that there were shepherds living in the fields, keeping watch over their flock, when an angel of the Lord stood before them, and the glory of the Lord shone around them, and they were terrified. But the angel said to them, "Do not be afraid; for see—I am bringing you good news of great joy for all the people: to you is born this day in the city of David a Savior, who is the Messiah, the Lord. This will be a sign for you: you will find a child wrapped in bands of cloth and lying in a manger." And suddenly there was with the angel a multitude of the heavenly host, praising God and saying, "Glory to God in the highest heaven, and on earth peace among those whom he favors!"

Christmas Day (Year B)

LECTIONARY READINGS

Isaiah 52:7–10
Psalm 98
Hebrews 1:1–12
John 1:1–14

CALL TO WORSHIP

Psalm 98:1–3

O sing to the Lord a new song, for he has done marvelous things. His right hand and his holy arm have gotten him victory. The Lord has made known his victory; he has revealed his vindication in the sight of the nations.
**He has remembered his steadfast love and faithfulness to the house of Israel.
All the ends of the earth have seen the victory of our God.**

PRAYER OF ADORATION

Based on Hebrews 1:1–4

Holy God, long ago you spoke to your people
in many and various ways by the prophets,
but in these last days you have spoken to us by your Son,
whom you appointed heir of all things,
through whom you also created the worlds.
Lord Jesus, you are the reflection of the Father's glory
and the exact imprint of his very being,
and you sustain all things by your powerful word.
When you had made purification for our sins,
you sat down at the Father's right hand,
where, even now, you are interceding on our behalf.
Praise to you, our Lord and King forever. Amen.

AFFIRMATION OF FAITH

Based on John 1:1–5, 14

What do we believe concerning Jesus as the Word?

We believe that in the beginning was the Word, and the Word was with God, and the Word was God. He was in the beginning with God.
All things came into being through him, and without him not one thing came into being.
We believe that what has come into being in him was life, and the life was the light of all people. The light shines in the darkness, and the darkness did not overcome it.
We believe that the Word became flesh and lived among us,
and we have seen his glory, the glory as of a father's only son, full of grace and truth.

First Sunday after Christmas (Year B)

LECTIONARY READINGS

Isaiah 61:10–62:3
Psalm 148
Galatians 4:4–7
Luke 2:22–40

CALL TO WORSHIP

Psalm 148:1–4, 13

Praise the Lord from the heavens; praise him in the heights!
Praise him, all his angels; praise him, all his host!
Praise him, sun and moon; praise him, all you shining stars!
Praise him, you highest heavens, and you waters above the heavens!
Let them praise the name of the Lord,
for his name alone is exalted; his glory is above earth and heaven.

PRAYER OF ADORATION

Based on Luke 2:25–35; Psalm 148:11–13

Merciful God,
with Simeon, we praise you for the salvation
which you prepared in the presence of all peoples,
a light for revelation to the gentiles
and for glory to your people Israel.
Though many oppose you,
the deepest thoughts of many hearts are revealed.
May all the peoples praise you, O Lord:
kings, princes, and all rulers of the earth;
young men and women alike, old and young together!

Let them praise the name of the Lord, for your name alone is exalted;
your glory is above earth and heaven. Amen.

AFFIRMATION OF FAITH

Based on Galatians 4:4–7

What do we believe concerning the birth of Jesus and our adoption as children of God?

We believe that when the fullness of time had come, God sent his Son, born of a woman, born under the law, in order to redeem those who were under the law.
We believe he did this so that we might receive adoption as children. And because we are children, God has sent the Spirit of his Son into our hearts, crying, "Abba! Father!"
Therefore, we believe we are no longer slaves but children,
and if children then also heirs, through God.

Second Sunday after Christmas (Year B)

LECTIONARY READINGS

Jeremiah 31:7–14
Psalm 147:12–20
Ephesians 1:3–14
John 1:1–18

CALL TO WORSHIP

Psalm 147:12–14

Praise the Lord, O Jerusalem! Praise your God, O Zion!
For he strengthens the bars of your gates;
he blesses your children within you.
He grants peace within your borders; he fills you with the finest of wheat.

PRAYER OF ADORATION

Based on Ephesians 1:3–8

Gracious God, we praise you, for you have blessed us in Christ
with every spiritual blessing in the heavenly places,
and chose us in Christ before the foundation of the world
to be holy and blameless before you in love.
You predestined us for adoption as your children
through Jesus Christ, according to the good pleasure of your will,
to the praise of your glorious grace that you freely bestowed on us.
In you we have redemption through your blood, the forgiveness of our trespasses, according to the riches of your grace that you lavished on us. Amen.

AFFIRMATION OF FAITH

Based on John 1:1–5, 14

What do we believe concerning the deity of Christ, the Word of God?

We believe that in the beginning was the Word,
and the Word was with God, and the Word was God.
We believe that he was in the beginning with God,
that all things came into being through him,
and without him not one thing came into being.
We believe that in him was life, and the life was the light of all people.
The light shines in the darkness, and the darkness did not overcome it.
We believe that the Word became flesh and lived among us,
and that we have seen his glory, the glory as of a father's only son, full of grace and truth.

Epiphany of the Lord (Year B)

LECTIONARY READINGS

Isaiah 60:1–6
Psalm 72:1–7, 10–14
Ephesians 3:1–12
Matthew 2:1–12

CALL TO WORSHIP

Psalm 72:1–2

Give the king your justice, O God,
and your righteousness to a king's son.
**May he judge your people with righteousness,
and your poor with justice.**

PRAYER OF ADORATION

Based on Isaiah 60:1–6

Child of Bethlehem,
we worship you, for your light has come,
and the glory of the Lord has risen upon you.
Nations came to your light,
and kings to the brightness of your dawn.
The wise men came to you;
the wealth of the nations came to worship and adore you.
They brought gold and frankincense,
and proclaimed the praise of the Lord.
We bow our knees to you, the King of kings and Lord of lords. Amen.

AFFIRMATION OF FAITH

Based on Matthew 2:1–2, 7–11

What do we believe concerning the visit of the Wise Men?

We believe that in the time of King Herod, after Jesus was born in Bethlehem of Judea, wise men from the East came to Jerusalem, asking, "Where is the child who has been born king of the Jews? For we observed his star at its rising, and have come to pay him homage."
We believe that Herod sent them to Bethlehem, saying, "Go and search diligently for the child; and when you have found him, bring me word so that I may also go and pay him homage."
We believe that when they had heard the king, they set out; and there, ahead of them, went the star that they had seen at its rising, until it stopped over the place where the child was. When they saw that the star had stopped, they were overwhelmed with joy. On entering the house, they saw the child with Mary his mother; and they knelt down and paid him homage. Then, opening their treasure chests, they offered him gifts of gold, frankincense, and myrrh.

Baptism of the Lord (Year B)

LECTIONARY READINGS

Genesis 1:1–5
Psalm 29
Acts 19:1–7
Mark 1:4–11

CALL TO WORSHIP

Psalm 29:1–4

Ascribe to the Lord, O heavenly beings,
ascribe to the Lord glory and strength.
Ascribe to the Lord the glory of his name;
worship the Lord in holy splendor.
The voice of the Lord is over the waters;
the God of glory thunders, the Lord, over mighty waters.
The voice of the Lord is powerful;
the voice of the Lord is full of majesty.

PRAYER OF RENEWAL

Based on Genesis 1:3; Acts 19:5–6; Mark 1:8

Creator God,
the one who said,
"Let there be light," and there was light,
bring new life into the darkness of our hearts.
As those baptized in the name of Jesus,
and regenerated by the power of the Holy Spirit,
we ask you to cleanse
and sanctify us from sin and idolatry.

In humility, may we turn to you in our time of need.
In the name of Jesus we pray. Amen.

AFFIRMATION OF FAITH

Based on Acts 19:4

What do we believe concerning John's baptism?

We believe John baptized with the baptism of repentance,
telling the people to believe in the one who was to come after him, that is,
in Jesus.

Second Sunday after Epiphany (Year B)

LECTIONARY READINGS

1 Samuel 3:1–20
Psalm 139: 1–6, 13–18
1 Corinthians 6:12–20
John 1:43–51

CALL TO WORSHIP

Psalm 139:1–3, 13–14

O Lord, you have searched me and known me.
You know when I sit down and when I rise up;
you discern my thoughts from far away.
You search out my path and my lying down,
and are acquainted with all my ways.
For it was you who formed my inward parts;
you knit me together in my mother's womb.
I praise you, for I am fearfully and wonderfully made.
Wonderful are your works; that I know very well.

PRAYER OF RENEWAL

Based on 1 Samuel 3:10; Psalm 139:14; 1 Corinthians 6:12, 19–20; John 1:45–46

Lord Jesus,
we thank you that we know you, and that we are known by you.
Truly, we are fearfully and wonderfully made.
Help us to steward our thoughts and our actions;
may all that we do be pleasing to you and beneficial to our souls.
By your grace, help us to extend the invitation of knowing you

to those around us: friends, family, neighbors, and those in need.
Renew the joy of being your disciples and help us to listen for your still small voice, leading and guiding us in all our ways.
In the name of Jesus we pray. Amen.

AFFIRMATION OF FAITH

Based on 1 Corinthians 6:17–20

What do we believe concerning our bodies and our union with Christ?

We believe that anyone united to the Lord becomes one spirit with him.
We believe we are to shun fornication, for every sin that a person commits is outside the body; but the fornicator sins against the body itself.
We believe that our body is a temple of the Holy Spirit within us,
which we have from God, and that we are not our own.
We believe that we were bought with a price; therefore we are to glorify God in our body.

Third Sunday after Epiphany (Year B)

LECTIONARY READINGS

Jonah 3:1–5, 10
Psalm 62:5–12
1 Corinthians 7:29–31
Mark 1:14–20

CALL TO WORSHIP

Psalm 62:5–7

For God alone my soul waits in silence,
for my hope is from him.
He alone is my rock and my salvation,
my fortress; I shall not be shaken.
On God rests my deliverance and my honor;
my mighty rock, my refuge is in God.

PRAYER OF RENEWAL

Based on Jonah 3:1–5, 10; Mark 1:16–20

Lord Jesus,
you call us to share the good news of the gospel,
but sometimes, like Jonah, we are reluctant to obey.
You call us to let go of earthly attachments and follow you,
but too often we want to hold on to our possessions and comforts in this life.
Sanctify us, O Lord, that our grip on this world would become less and less,
and our desire to obey you in all circumstances would become more and
more. In the name of Jesus we pray. Amen.

AFFIRMATION OF FAITH

Based on Mark 1:16–20

What do we believe concerning the calling of the first disciples?

We believe that as Jesus passed along the Sea of Galilee,
he saw Simon and his brother Andrew casting a net into the sea—for they were fishermen.
We believe that Jesus said to them, "Follow me and I will make you fish for people."
And immediately they left their nets and followed him.
We believe that as he went a little farther, he saw James son of Zebedee
and his brother John, who were in their boat mending the nets.
We believe he called them; and they left their father Zebedee
in the boat with the hired men, and followed him.

Fourth Sunday after Epiphany (Year B)

LECTIONARY READINGS

Deuteronomy 18:15–20
Psalm 111
1 Corinthians 8:1–13
Mark 1:21–28

CALL TO WORSHIP

Psalm 111:1–2, 9–10

I will give thanks to the Lord with my whole heart,
in the company of the upright, in the congregation.
Great are the works of the Lord,
studied by all who delight in them.
He sent redemption to his people;
he has commanded his covenant forever.
Holy and awesome is his name.
The fear of the Lord is the beginning of wisdom;
all those who practice it have a good understanding.
His praise endures forever.

PRAYER OF ADORATION

Based on Mark 1:21–28; 1 Corinthians 8:6

Lord Jesus,
you are our true Prophet, Priest, and King.
When you speak the raging waters are stilled,
the blind receive sight, and the dead are brought back to life.
We worship and adore you, the Holy One of God,
in whom are all things and through whom we exist. Amen.

AFFIRMATION OF FAITH

Based on 1 Corinthians 8:1, 12–13

What do we believe concerning love and knowledge?

We believe that knowledge puffs up, but love builds up.

What do we believe concerning differences of opinion among one another?

We believe that when we sin against a brother or a sister in the Lord and wound his or her conscience when it is weak, we sin against Christ. Therefore, if something causes another brother or sister in Christ to stumble, we should refrain from doing it, so that we may not cause one of them to fall.

Fifth Sunday after Epiphany (Year B)

LECTIONARY READINGS

Isaiah 40:21–31
Psalm 147:1–11, 20
1 Corinthians 9:16–23
Mark 1:29–39

CALL TO WORSHIP

Psalm 147:1–5

Praise the Lord! How good it is to sing praises to our God;
for he is gracious, and a song of praise is fitting.
The Lord builds up Jerusalem; he gathers the outcasts of Israel.
He heals the brokenhearted, and binds up their wounds.
He determines the number of the stars; he gives to all of them their names.
Great is our Lord, and abundant in power; his understanding is beyond measure.

PRAYER OF RENEWAL

Based on Isaiah 40:28–29, 31; Mark 1:29–39

Lord Jesus,
you are the everlasting God,
the Creator of the ends of the earth.
You do not grow weary; your understanding is unsearchable.
While on earth, you healed the sick, cast out demons,
and proclaimed the good news of salvation to all with ears to hear.
In our weariness, give us strength;
in our weakness, make us strong.
By your grace, help us to mount up with wings like eagles,
never tiring in our labor for the kingdom; never shying away

from sharing your grace and mercy to those around us.
This we ask in the strong name of Jesus. Amen.

AFFIRMATION OF FAITH

Based on Isaiah 40:28–31

What do we believe concerning the strength and compassion of the Lord?

We believe the Lord is the everlasting God, the Creator of the ends of the earth. He does not faint or grow weary; his understanding is unsearchable. We believe he gives power to the faint, and strengthens the powerless. Even youths will faint and be weary, and the young will fall exhausted; but we believe that those who wait for the Lord
shall renew their strength, they shall mount up with wings like eagles, they shall run and not be weary, they shall walk and not faint.

Sixth Sunday after Epiphany (Year B)

LECTIONARY READINGS

2 Kings 5:1–14
Psalm 30
1 Corinthians 9:24–27
Mark 1:40–45

CALL TO WORSHIP

Psalm 30:4–5

Sing praises to the Lord, O you his faithful ones,
and give thanks to his holy name.
For his anger is but for a moment; his favor is for a lifetime.
Weeping may linger for the night, but joy comes with the morning.

PRAYER OF RENEWAL

Based on Mark 1:40–45

Lord Jesus,
come to us in your mercy and make us whole.
Like those who were afflicted,
to whom you stretched out your hand,
may we receive your healing touch,
breaking the bonds of sin which too easily entangle us.
By your grace, may we share your love
and power with those around us.
May they know the freedom that only you can bring.
In the name of Jesus we pray. Amen.

AFFIRMATION OF FAITH

Based on 1 Corinthians 9:24–27

What do we believe concerning a life of self-control, above reproach?

We believe that, like runners competing in a race,
we are to run in such a way that we may win the prize.
We believe that athletes exercise self-control in all things;
they do it to receive a perishable wreath, but we an imperishable one.
Therefore, we do not run aimlessly, nor do we box as though beating the air;
but we discipline our bodies and keep them under control,
so that after proclaiming to others we ourselves should not be disqualified.

Seventh Sunday after Epiphany (Year B)

LECTIONARY READINGS

Isaiah 43:18–25
Psalm 41
2 Corinthians 1:18–22
Mark 2:1–12

CALL TO WORSHIP

Psalm 41:1–3

Happy are those who consider the poor;
the Lord delivers them in the day of trouble.
**The Lord protects them and keeps them alive;
they are called happy in the land.
You do not give them up to the will of their enemies.**
The Lord sustains them on their sickbed;
in their illness you heal all their infirmities.

PRAYER OF RENEWAL

Based on Mark 2:1–12

Lord Jesus, we are desperate for you.
Give us faith to turn to you
and cry out to you in our time of need.
We confess that, too often, we remain in isolation,
wanting to protect our name and our reputation;
but only you can truly heal us, physically and spiritually.
In your mercy, expose us,
and give us the grace to go to any length
to draw closer and closer to you,
seeking the power of your name to restore us.

And may all be amazed and glorify you, saying,
"We have never seen anything like this!"
In the name of Jesus we pray. Amen.

AFFIRMATION OF FAITH

Based on 2 Corinthians 1:20–22

What do we believe concerning God's promises and our identity in Christ?

We believe that every one of God's promises is a "Yes."
For this reason it is through him that we say the "Amen," to the glory of God.
We believe that it is God who establishes us together in Christ and has anointed us,
by putting his seal on us and giving us his Spirit in our hearts as a first installment.

Eighth Sunday after Epiphany (Year B)

LECTIONARY READINGS

Hosea 2:14–20
Psalm 103:1–13, 22
2 Corinthians 3:1–6
Mark 2:13–22

CALL TO WORSHIP

Psalm 103:11–13

For as the heavens are high above the earth,
so great is his steadfast love toward those who fear him;
as far as the east is from the west,
so far he removes our transgressions from us.
As a father has compassion for his children,
so the Lord has compassion for those who fear him.

PRAYER OF RENEWAL

Based on Mark 2:13–17

Lord Jesus,
you call us to follow you;
to lay aside our own agendas
and seek your kingdom.
Like Levi, we want to find ourselves
surrounded by others who have sought
and found your grace and forgiveness.
Help us to come as we are, but not stay as we are.
Transform us and give us a heart for this broken world,
reaching out in love to those who need your grace and mercy.
In the name of Jesus we pray. Amen.

AFFIRMATION OF FAITH

Based on 2 Corinthians 3:3

What do we believe concerning our testimony to the world?

We believe that we are a letter of Christ, written not with ink
but with the Spirit of the living God,
not on tablets of stone but on tablets of human hearts.

Ninth Sunday after Epiphany (Year B)

LECTIONARY READINGS

Deuteronomy 5:12–15
Psalm 81:1–10
2 Corinthians 4:5–12
Mark 2:23–3:6

CALL TO WORSHIP

Psalm 81:1–2

Sing aloud to God our strength;
shout for joy to the God of Jacob.
Raise a song, sound the tambourine,
the sweet lyre with the harp.

PRAYER OF RENEWAL

Based on Deuteronomy 5:12–14; 2 Corinthians 4:7–11

Holy God,
you have woven into our very being
the rhythm of one day in seven for rest, for sabbath.
May we see this as a life-giving ordinance
for worship and for the renewal of our souls.
Give us strength, for we are only fragile jars of clay.
Remind us that all power comes from you and not ourselves.
Though we face trials and afflictions, we are not crushed;
though we may feel confused and perplexed, we do not despair;
though we may experience persecution, you are always with us.
Help us put to death all that is not pleasing to you,
so that the life of Christ may become more and more evident in us. Amen.

AFFIRMATION OF FAITH

Based on Deuteronomy 5:12–14; Mark 2:27–28; 3:4–5

What do we believe concerning the Sabbath?

We believe God created a rhythm in creation—one day in seven for sabbath rest.
We believe the Sabbath was made for humankind, and not humankind for the Sabbath.
We further affirm that the Son of Man is Lord even of the Sabbath.
We believe the sabbath brings us opportunities
to do good and not harm; to bring life, not destroy it.

Transfiguration of the Lord (Year B)

LECTIONARY READINGS

2 Kings 2:1–12
Psalm 50:1–6
2 Corinthians 4:3–6
Mark 9:2–9

CALL TO WORSHIP

Psalm 50:1–2

The mighty one, God the Lord, speaks and summons the earth from the rising of the sun to its setting.
Out of Zion, the perfection of beauty, God shines forth.

PRAYER OF ADORATION

Based on Mark 9:2–9; 2 Corinthians 4:6

Triune God,
in the mystery of the transfiguration,
we are given a glimpse of your glory,
and we bow in worship and adoration.
We behold your majesty and power
as we hear the Father's voice from heaven, saying:
"This is my Son, the Beloved; listen to him!"
Holy Spirit, open our eyes that we may see
the knowledge of the glory of God in the face of Jesus Christ,
in whose name we pray. Amen.

AFFIRMATION OF FAITH

Based on 2 Corinthians 4:3–4, 6

What do we believe concerning the gospel and the knowledge of God?

We believe that if the gospel is veiled, it is veiled to those who are perishing.
We believe that, in their case as unbelievers,
the god of this world has blinded their minds,
to keep them from seeing the light of the gospel of the glory of Christ,
who is the image of God.
But we believe it is the God who said, "Let light shine out of darkness,"
who has shone in our hearts, as believers, to give us the light of the knowledge
of the glory of God in the face of Jesus Christ.

Ash Wednesday (Year B)

LECTIONARY READINGS

Joel 2:1–2, 12–17
Psalm 51:1–17
2 Corinthians 5:20b–6:10
Matthew 6:1–6, 16–21

CALL TO WORSHIP

Psalm 51:15–17

O Lord, open my lips,
and my mouth will declare your praise.
For you have no delight in sacrifice;
if I were to give a burnt offering, you would not be pleased.
The sacrifice acceptable to God is a broken spirit;
a broken and contrite heart, O God, you will not despise.

PRAYER OF RENEWAL

Based on Matthew 6:1–6, 16–21

Gracious God,
help us not to be hypocrites in our faith,
wanting to be seen and approved by others
more than to find our reward in you alone.
When we give, may we not let our left hand
know what our right hand is doing;
when we pray, may we go into our room
and shut the door and pray to you in secret;
when we fast, may we not look dismal and distressed,
but may we have a clean appearance
so that our fasting is not obvious to anyone.

Regarding material things, may we store up for ourselves treasures in heaven, where neither moth nor rust consumes and where thieves do not break in and steal. For where our treasure is, there our heart will be also.
In the name of Jesus we pray. Amen.

AFFIRMATION OF FAITH

Based on 2 Corinthians 6:1–2

What do we believe concerning the grace of God and the urgency of salvation?

We believe we are not to accept the grace of God in vain. For he says,
"At an acceptable time I have listened to you, and on a day of salvation I have helped you."
Therefore, we believe that now is the acceptable time; now is the day of salvation!

First Sunday in Lent (Year B)

LECTIONARY READINGS

Genesis 9:8–17
Psalm 25:1–10
1 Peter 3:18–22
Mark 1:9–15

CALL TO WORSHIP

Psalm 25:1, 8–10

To you, O Lord, I lift up my soul.
Good and upright is the Lord; therefore he instructs sinners in the way.
He leads the humble in what is right, and teaches the humble his way.
All the paths of the Lord are steadfast love and faithfulness,
for those who keep his covenant and his decrees.

PRAYER OF RENEWAL

Based on Psalm 25:5–7; Mark 1:12–13

Holy God, we thank you for keeping your covenant with us,
for you are a God of mercy and steadfast love
who does not remember the sins of our youth or our transgressions.
By your grace, would you lead us in your truth,
and teach us, for you are the God of our salvation.
As you were sustained in the wilderness for forty days,
may we be filled with the Spirit when the enemy tempts us.
Protect us and keep us that we would follow you and flee from sin.
In the name of Jesus we pray. Amen.

AFFIRMATION OF FAITH

Based on 1 Peter 3:18–22

What do we believe regarding our salvation and baptism?

We believe that Christ suffered for sins once for all,
the righteous for the unrighteous, in order to bring us to God.
We believe that he was put to death in the flesh, but made alive in the spirit,
in which also he went and made a proclamation to the spirits in prison,
who in former times did not obey, when God waited patiently in the days of Noah,
during the building of the ark, in which a few, that is, eight persons, were saved through water.
We believe that baptism, which the flood prefigured, now saves us—
not as a removal of dirt from the body, but as an appeal to God for a good conscience,
through the resurrection of Jesus Christ, who has gone into heaven
and is at the right hand of God, with angels, authorities, and powers made subject to him.

Second Sunday in Lent (Year B)

LECTIONARY READINGS

Genesis 17:1–7, 15–16
Psalm 22:23–31
Romans 4:13–25
Mark 8:31–38

CALL TO WORSHIP

Psalm 22:27–28

All the ends of the earth shall remember and turn to the Lord;
and all the families of the nations shall worship before him.
For dominion belongs to the Lord, and he rules over the nations.

PRAYER OF RENEWAL

Based on Romans 4:18–21; Mark 8:34–35

Sovereign God, the covenants with your people stand forever.
We praise you for your faithfulness and for keeping your promises
to Abraham and all of his descendants, our spiritual family.
Strengthen our faith, O Lord, and help us to place our trust in you.
Empowered by the Spirit, may we hope against hope
and give glory to you, even in desperate circumstances.
Help us to deny ourselves and take up our cross and follow you.
For we know that those who want to save their life will lose it,
and those who lose their life for your sake, and for the sake of the gospel,
will save it. In the name of Jesus we pray. Amen.

AFFIRMATION OF FAITH

Based on Romans 4:13, 22–25

What do we believe concerning the law, the promise, and the righteousness of faith?

We believe that the promise that Abraham would inherit the world did not come to him or to his descendants through the law but through the righteousness of faith.
We believe that Abraham's faith "was reckoned to him as righteousness." We also believe that the words, "it was reckoned to him," were written not for his sake alone, but for ours also. It will be reckoned to us who believe in him who raised Jesus our Lord from the dead, who was handed over to death for our trespasses and was raised for our justification.

Third Sunday in Lent (Year B)

LECTIONARY READINGS

Exodus 20:1–17
Psalm 19
1 Corinthians 1:18–25
John 2:13–22

CALL TO WORSHIP

Psalm 19:1–4

The heavens are telling the glory of God;
and the firmament proclaims his handiwork.
Day to day pours forth speech,
and night to night declares knowledge.
There is no speech, nor are there words;
their voice is not heard;
Yet their voice goes out through all the earth,
and their words to the end of the world.

PRAYER OF RENEWAL

Based on Psalm 19:7–8, 10; 1 Corinthians 1:18

Holy God, your law is perfect, reviving the soul;
your decrees are sure, making wise the simple.
Help us to follow your ways, that our hearts may rejoice,
and keep your commandments, that our eyes may be enlightened.
May we desire your word more than gold,
and find all within it sweeter than honey.
By your grace, may we be led by the Spirit,
following the truth of the gospel and not the wisdom of this world;
for we know that the message of the cross is foolishness

to those who are perishing, but to us who are being saved it is the power of God. In the name of Jesus we pray. Amen.

AFFIRMATION OF FAITH

Based on 1 Corinthians 1:18, 25

What do we believe concerning the message of the cross?

We believe that the message about the cross is foolishness to those who are perishing, but to us who are being saved it is the power of God.
We believe that God's foolishness is wiser than human wisdom,
and God's weakness is stronger than human strength.

Fourth Sunday in Lent (Year B)

LECTIONARY READINGS

Numbers 21:4–9
Psalm 107:1–3, 17–22
Ephesians 2:1–10
John 3:14–21

CALL TO WORSHIP

Psalm 107:1

O give thanks to the Lord, for he is good;
for his steadfast love endures forever.

PRAYER OF RENEWAL

Based on John 3:14–15, 20–21

Lord Jesus,
just as Moses lifted up the serpent in the wilderness,
so you were lifted up, that whoever believes in you may have eternal life.
Our desire, O Lord, is to follow you and experience that abundant, eternal life now, but we confess that we often fall short and go our own way.
When we sin, may the Spirit help us to come to the light and confess our wrongs so that our deeds may be exposed and our hearts may be healed.
In the name of Jesus we pray. Amen.

AFFIRMATION OF FAITH

Based on Ephesians 2:1–2, 4–10

What do we believe about sin, grace, and good works?

We believe that we were dead through the trespasses and sins in which we once lived,
following the course of this world, following the ruler of the power of the air, the spirit that is now at work among those who are disobedient.
But we believe that God, who is rich in mercy,
out of the great love with which he loved us even when we were dead through our trespasses,
made us alive together with Christ and raised us up with him
and seated us with him in the heavenly places in Christ Jesus, so that in the ages to come
he might show the immeasurable riches of his grace in kindness toward us in Christ Jesus.
We believe it is by grace we have been saved through faith, and this is not our own doing;
it is the gift of God—not the result of works, so that no one may boast.
We believe that we are what he has made us, created in Christ Jesus for good works, which God prepared beforehand to be our way of life.

Fifth Sunday in Lent (Year B)

LECTIONARY READINGS

Jeremiah 31:31–34
Psalm 51:1–12
Hebrews 5:5–10
John 12:20–33

CALL TO WORSHIP

Jeremiah 31:31, 33

The days are surely coming, says the Lord,
when I will make a new covenant
with the house of Israel and the house of Judah.
I will put my law within them, and I will write it on their hearts;
and I will be their God, and they shall be my people.

PRAYER OF RENEWAL

Based on Jeremiah 31:31, 33; Psalm 51:1–2; Hebrews 5:5–6

Lord Jesus,
you are our covenant-keeping God, and we are your people.
We praise you that you have put your law within us,
but we confess that, too often, we quench your Spirit
and go against the law that is written on our hearts.
Have mercy on us, O God, according to your steadfast love;
according to your abundant mercy blot out our transgressions.
Thank you, Lord, that as our high priest, you continue to intercede for us,
and through the Spirit, you continue to wash us and cleanse us from our sin.
In the name of Jesus we pray. Amen.

AFFIRMATION OF FAITH

Based on Hebrews 5:5–6

What do we believe concerning Christ's office of high priest?

We believe that Christ did not glorify himself in becoming a high priest,
but was appointed by the one who said to him,
"You are my Son, today I have begotten you";
as he says also in another place,
"You are a priest forever, according to the order of Melchizedek."

Palm Sunday (Year B)

LECTIONARY READINGS

Mark 11:1–11
Psalm 118:1–2, 19–29

CALL TO WORSHIP

Psalm 118:1, 26

O give thanks to the Lord, for he is good;
his steadfast love endures forever!
Blessed is the one who comes in the name of the Lord.
We bless you from the house of the Lord.

PRAYER OF ADORATION

Based on Psalm 118:21–23, 26; Mark 11:7–11

Lord Jesus,
on this Palm Sunday we worship you
and join our voices with those from long ago, saying,
"Blessed is the one who comes in the name of the Lord."
Though you were rejected by your own people,
you have become the chief cornerstone.
As you rode into Jerusalem, you rode on to die and have become our salvation.
This was all according to your sovereign plan, and it is marvelous in our eyes.
In the name of Jesus we pray. Amen.

AFFIRMATION OF FAITH

Based on Mark 11:7–10

What do we believe concerning Jesus' triumphal entry into Jerusalem?

We believe the disciples brought a colt to Jesus and threw their cloaks on it; and he sat on it.
We believe that many people spread their cloaks on the road, and others spread leafy branches that they had cut in the fields. Then those who went ahead and those who followed were shouting,
"Hosanna! Blessed is the one who comes in the name of the Lord!
Blessed is the coming kingdom of our ancestor David!
Hosanna in the highest heaven!"

Maundy Thursday (Year B)

LECTIONARY READINGS

Exodus 12:1–14
Psalm 116:1–2, 12–19
1 Corinthians 11:23–26
John 13:1–17, 31b–35

CALL TO WORSHIP

Psalm 116:1–2

I love the Lord, because he has heard
my voice and my supplications.
**Because he inclined his ear to me,
therefore I will call on him as long as I live.**

PRAYER OF RENEWAL

Based on 1 Corinthians 11:23–26

Lord Jesus,
may we live in remembrance of you
and all that you have done for us.
We thank you for the meal which you have given us,
through which we receive your grace.
In the breaking of the bread,
may we know it is your body, which is for us.
When we take the cup, may we know it is the new covenant in your blood.
For as often as we eat the bread and drink the cup,
we proclaim your death until you come again.
In the name of Jesus we pray. Amen.

AFFIRMATION OF FAITH

Based on John 13:1, 5, 15–17

What do we believe concerning Jesus' example of servanthood?

We believe that, before the festival of the Passover,
Jesus poured water into a basin, washed the disciples' feet,
and wiped them with the towel that was tied around him.
We believe that Jesus set an example for us,
that we should do as he has done for us.
We believe that servants are not greater than their master,
nor are messengers greater than the one who sent them.
We believe that, if we know these things, we are blessed if we do them.

Good Friday (Year B)

LECTIONARY READINGS

Isaiah 52:13–53:12
Psalm 22
Hebrews 4:14–16; 5:7–9
John 18:1–19:42

CALL TO WORSHIP

Isaiah 53:1–3

Who has believed what we have heard? And to whom has the arm of the Lord been revealed
For he grew up before him like a young plant, and like a root out of dry ground; he had no form or majesty that we should look at him, nothing in his appearance that we should desire him.
He was despised and rejected by others; a man of suffering and acquainted with infirmity; and as one from whom others hide their faces he was despised, and we held him of no account.

PRAYER OF ADORATION

Based on Hebrews 4:15–16; 5:7, 9

Lord Jesus,
in you, we do not have a high priest
who is unable to sympathize with our weaknesses,
but we have one who in every respect
has been tested as we are, yet without sin.
Out of love, you invite us to approach the throne of grace with boldness,
so that we may receive mercy and find grace to help in time of need.
We praise you, for when you walked this earth,
you offered up prayers and supplications, with loud cries and tears,

to the one who was able to save you from death,
and you have become the source of eternal salvation for all who obey you.
In the name of Jesus we pray. Amen.

AFFIRMATION OF FAITH

Based on John 19:28–30

What do we believe concerning the death of our Lord?

We believe that when Jesus knew that all was finished,
he said (in order to fulfill the scripture), "I am thirsty."
We believe that a jar full of sour wine was standing there.
So they put a sponge full of the wine on a branch of hyssop and held it to his mouth.
We believe that when Jesus had received the wine,
he said, "It is finished." Then he bowed his head and gave up his spirit.

Easter (Year B)

LECTIONARY READINGS

Acts 10:34–43
Psalm 118:1–2, 14–24
1 Corinthians 15:1–11
Mark 16:1–8

CALL TO WORSHIP

Psalm 118:1, 22–24

O give thanks to the Lord, for he is good; his steadfast love endures forever!
The stone that the builders rejected has become the chief cornerstone.
This is the Lord's doing; it is marvelous in our eyes.
This is the day that the Lord has made; let us rejoice and be glad in it.

PRAYER OF RENEWAL

Based on Mark 16:4–6; 1 Corinthians 15:3–4; Acts 10:43

Lord Jesus, on this Easter Sunday we celebrate
the joy of the resurrection and the reality of the empty tomb.
We praise you that you died for our sins, that you were buried,
and that you were raised on the third day in accordance with the Scriptures.
May these truths provide fuel for our faith
and boldness to proclaim the good news
that anyone who believes in Christ
receives forgiveness of sins through his name.
Thank you for this message of hope and new life.
In the name of Jesus we pray. Amen.

AFFIRMATION OF FAITH

Based on Acts 10:38–41, 43

What do we believe concerning the gospel message that spread throughout Judea, beginning in Galilee after the baptism that John announced?

We believe that God anointed Jesus of Nazareth with the Holy Spirit and with power and that he went about doing good and healing all who were oppressed by the devil, for God was with him.
We believe he was put to death, being hanged on a tree, but God raised him on the third day and allowed him to appear, not to all the people, but to those who were chosen by God as witnesses, and who ate and drank with him after he rose from the dead.
We believe that all the prophets testify about him that everyone who believes in him receives forgiveness of sins through his name.

Second Sunday of Easter (Year B)

LECTIONARY READINGS

Acts 4:32–35
Psalm 133
1 John 1:1–2:2
John 20:19–31

CALL TO WORSHIP

Psalm 133:1

How very good and pleasant it is
when kindred live together in unity!

PRAYER OF RENEWAL

Based on Acts 4:33–35; 1 John 2:1–2; John 20:26–29

Lord Jesus,
your great grace was upon the early followers
and there was not a needy person among them.
Help us to be gracious in our care for one another,
giving of our time and treasure with joyful hearts,
for we often have our eyes only on ourselves.
When, like Thomas, we doubt the testimonies about you,
give us faith to believe in your resurrection power.
In all of our shortcomings, O Lord, we thank you
that we have an advocate in Jesus Christ,
and that he is the atoning sacrifice for our sins,
and not for ours only but also for the sins of the whole world.
In the name of Jesus we pray. Amen.

AFFIRMATION OF FAITH

Based on 1 John 1:5–10

What do we believe concerning the confession of our sins and our fellowship with the Lord and with one another?

We believe that God is light and in him there is no darkness at all.
We believe that if we say that we have fellowship with him while we are walking in darkness,
we lie and do not do what is true; but if we walk in the light as he himself is in the light,
we have fellowship with one another, and the blood of Jesus his Son cleanses us from all sin.
We believe that if we say that we have no sin, we deceive ourselves, and the truth is not in us.
We believe that if we confess our sins, he who is faithful and just will forgive us our sins
and cleanse us from all unrighteousness. However, if we say that we have not sinned, we make him a liar, and his word is not in us.

Third Sunday of Easter (Year B)

LECTIONARY READINGS

Acts 3:12–19
Psalm 4
1 John 3:1–7
Luke 24:36b–48

CALL TO WORSHIP

1 John 3:1

See what love the Father has given us,
that we should be called children of God;
and that is what we are.

PRAYER OF RENEWAL

Based on Acts 3:16; 1 John 3:5; Luke 24:44–47

Lord Jesus,
we know that your name is powerful,
able to heal us and make us whole.
As your children, breathe fresh faith into our broken lives:
where we are weak, make us strong;
where we doubt, give us assurance;
where we have sinned, grant us forgiveness.
Help us to believe that everything written about you
in the law of Moses, the prophets, and the psalms must be fulfilled.
By your Spirit, open our hearts and minds to understand the Scriptures,
that you were to suffer and to rise from the dead on the third day;
that repentance and forgiveness of sins is
to be proclaimed in your name to all nations. Amen.

AFFIRMATION OF FAITH

Based on 1 John 3:2–3

What do we believe concerning our identity now and in the future?

We believe that we are God's children now;
what we will be has not yet been revealed.
We believe that when Christ is revealed,
we will be like him, for we will see him as he is.
And all who have this hope in him purify themselves, just as he is pure.

Fourth Sunday of Easter
(Good Shepherd Sunday, Year B)

LECTIONARY READINGS

Acts 4:5–12
Psalm 23
1 John 3:16–24
John 10:11–18

CALL TO WORSHIP

Psalm 23:1–3

The Lord is my shepherd, I shall not want.
He makes me lie down in green pastures;
he leads me beside still waters; he restores my soul.
He leads me in right paths for his name's sake.

PRAYER OF RENEWAL

Based on Psalm 23:1–4, 6; John 10:14–15

Lord Jesus,
you are our Good Shepherd,
leading us to quiet waters and restoring our souls.
You are with us in the darkest valley,
protecting us and comforting us in our time of need.
Out of love, you laid down your life for us
so that we could have intimate fellowship with you.
Help us to listen to and know your voice,
not the accusing and condemning voices that often assault us.
By your grace, may goodness and mercy follow us all the days of our lives.
In the name of Jesus we pray. Amen.

AFFIRMATION OF FAITH

Based on 1 John 3:18–20, 24

What do we believe concerning genuine love for one another?

We believe we are to love, not in word or speech, but in truth and action.
We believe that by this we will know that we are from the truth
and will reassure our hearts before him whenever our hearts condemn us;
for God is greater than our hearts, and he knows everything.
We believe that all who obey his commandments abide in him, and he abides in them.
And by this we know that he abides in us, by the Spirit that he has given us.

Fifth Sunday of Easter (Year B)

LECTIONARY READINGS

Acts 8:26–40
Psalm 22:25–31
1 John 4:7–21
John 15:1–8

CALL TO WORSHIP

Psalm 22:27–28

All the ends of the earth shall remember and turn to the Lord;
and all the families of the nations shall worship before him.
For dominion belongs to the Lord, and he rules over the nations.

PRAYER OF RENEWAL

Based on John 15:1–8

Lord God,
you are the vine and we are the branches;
teach us to abide in you throughout each new day.
Show us how to love our neighbors,
and give us a hunger for your word.
Prune all that leads us away from you
and the areas of our lives that do not bear fruit.
Guide us, we pray, through the abiding power and witness of your Spirit.
In the name of Jesus we pray. Amen.

AFFIRMATION OF FAITH

Based on 1 John 4:7–10, 13–16

Why are we called to love one another?

Because love is from God. Everyone who loves is born of God and knows God. Whoever does not love does not know God, for God is love.

How was God's love revealed among us?

God sent his only Son into the world so that we might live through him. In this is love, not that we loved God but that he loved us and sent his Son to be the atoning sacrifice for our sins.

How do we know that we abide in him and he in us?

Because he has given us of his Spirit. And we have seen and do testify that the Father has sent his Son as the Savior of the world. God abides in those who confess that Jesus is the Son of God, and they abide in God. So we have known and believe the love that God has for us. God is love, and those who abide in love abide in God, and God abides in them.

Sixth Sunday of Easter (Year B)

LECTIONARY READINGS

Acts 10:44–48
Psalm 98
1 John 5:1–6
John 15:9–17

CALL TO WORSHIP

Psalm 98:1, 4–6

O sing to the Lord a new song, for he has done marvelous things.
Make a joyful noise to the Lord, all the earth;
break forth into joyous song and sing praises.
Sing praises to the Lord with the lyre,
with the lyre and the sound of melody.
With trumpets and the sound of the horn
make a joyful noise before the King, the Lord.

PRAYER OF RENEWAL

Based on John 15:9–17

Everlasting Father,
help us to keep your commandments and to abide in your love,
that our joy be complete in you.
Show us how to love others as we have been loved by you.
May we be willing to lay aside our own agendas and desires,
to sacrificially love and serve our neighbors and our friends.
We want to bear fruit that will last,
for your kingdom and for the glory of your name. Amen.

AFFIRMATION OF FAITH

Based on 1 John 5:2–3, 6

How do we demonstrate our love for the children of God?

We believe that we demonstrate our love for the children of God
when we love God and obey his commandments.

What do we believe concerning the testimony of Christ?

We believe that Jesus Christ came by water and blood.
We believe that the Spirit is the one that testifies, for the Spirit is the truth.

Ascension of the Lord (Year B)

LECTIONARY READINGS

Acts 1:1–11
Psalm 47
Ephesians 1:15–23
Luke 24:44–53

CALL TO WORSHIP

Psalm 47:1–2, 6–7

Clap your hands, all you peoples; shout to God with loud songs of joy.
For the Lord, the Most High, is awesome, a great king over all the earth.
Sing praises to God, sing praises; sing praises to our King, sing praises.
For God is the king of all the earth; sing praises with a psalm.

PRAYER OF RENEWAL

Based on Ephesians 1:17–21

Father God, we pray that you would give us
a spirit of wisdom and revelation as we come to know Christ,
so that, with the eyes of our heart enlightened,
we may know the hope to which you have called us,
the riches of Christ's glorious inheritance among the saints,
and the immeasurable greatness of Christ's power for us who believe.
We thank you that you put this power to work in Christ
when you raised him from the dead
and seated him at your right hand in the heavenly places,
far above all rule and authority and power and dominion,
and above every name that is named, not only in this age,
but also in the age to come. Amen.

AFFIRMATION OF FAITH

Based on Acts 1:3, 8, 11

What do we believe concerning Jesus' appearances to the apostles after the resurrection, his ascension, and our role as the church?

We believe that after he suffered, Jesus presented himself alive to the apostles by many convincing proofs, appearing to them during forty days and speaking about the kingdom of God.
We believe that, like the apostles, we receive power through the Holy Spirit, and that we, the church, are called to be Christ's witnesses to the ends of the earth.
We believe that Jesus, who was taken up to heaven,
will come again in the same way he departed.

Seventh Sunday of Easter (Year B)

LECTIONARY READINGS

Acts 1:15–17, 21–26
Psalm 1
1 John 5:9–13
John 17:6–19

CALL TO WORSHIP

Psalm 1:1–3

Happy are those who do not follow the advice of the wicked,
or take the path that sinners tread, or sit in the seat of scoffers;
but their delight is in the law of the Lord,
and on his law they meditate day and night.
**They are like trees planted by streams of water,
which yield their fruit in its season,
and their leaves do not wither. In all that they do, they prosper.**

PRAYER OF RENEWAL

Based on John 17:11–19

Lord Jesus, you intercede for us
and protect us, so that we may be one.
Though you returned to the Father, we know
you are present with us through the Holy Spirit,
and our joy is complete in you.
Give us the desire to feast on your word and guard us from the evil one.
Help us to remember that though we are in the world,
we are not to be of the world.
By your grace, send us as your ambassadors,
shining as light in the darkness.

Sanctify us in your truth; your word is truth.
In the name of Jesus we pray. Amen.

AFFIRMATION OF FAITH

Based on 1 John 5:9–12

What do we believe concerning the testimony of God?

We believe that if we receive human testimony, the testimony of God is greater; for this is the testimony of God that he has testified to his Son.
We believe that those who believe in the Son of God have the testimony in their hearts,
and those who do not believe in God have made him a liar by not believing in the testimony that God has given concerning his Son.
We believe this is the testimony: God gave us eternal life, and this life is in his Son.
Whoever has the Son has life; whoever does not have the Son of God does not have life.

Day of Pentecost (Year B)

LECTIONARY READINGS

Acts 2:1–21
Psalm 104:24–34, 35b
Romans 8:22–27
John 15:26–27; 16:4b–15

CALL TO WORSHIP

Psalm 104:24

O Lord, how manifold are your works!
**In wisdom you have made them all
the earth is full of your creatures.**

PRAYER OF RENEWAL

Based on Romans 8:22–27; John 15:26; 16:13

Holy Spirit,
be our Advocate and Helper today.
Help us in our weakness.
When our own prayers fall short,
intercede for us with sighs too deep for words.
Align our hearts with the will of the Father,
and give us hope for what we do not see.
Spirit of truth, guide us and fill us
with wisdom and revelation,
with power and illumination from your word.
May we rest in you for this day. Amen.

AFFIRMATION OF FAITH

Based on Acts 2:1–6

What do we believe concerning the Day of Pentecost?

We believe that on the day of Pentecost, fifty days after Jesus' resurrection,
there came from heaven a sound like the rush of a violent wind,
and it filled the entire house where the apostles were sitting.
We believe that divided tongues, as of fire, appeared among them,
and a tongue rested on each of them.
We believe that all of them were filled with the Holy Spirit
and began to speak in other languages, as the Spirit gave them ability.
We believe that Jews from every nation who were living in Jerusalem,
miraculously heard the apostles' message concerning God's deeds of power
in their own native language.

Trinity Sunday (Year B)

LECTIONARY READINGS

Isaiah 6:1–8
Psalm 29
Romans 8:12–17
John 3:1–17

CALL TO WORSHIP

Psalm 29:1–2

Ascribe to the Lord, O heavenly beings,
ascribe to the Lord glory and strength.
Ascribe to the Lord the glory of his name;
worship the Lord in holy splendor.

PRAYER OF RENEWAL

Based on Romans 8:12–17

God in Three Persons, Blessed Trinity;
we are grateful that we are part of your family, the Body of Christ.
May we not live according to the flesh,
but be led by your Spirit as your children.
Remove a spirit of slavery and fear and fill us with the spirit of adoption.
As we come to you, Abba Father,
may our hearts bear witness with the Spirit
that we are your sons and daughters.
Remind us that we are heirs of God
and joint heirs with Christ: that when we suffer with him
we will also be glorified with him.
In the name of the Father, Son, and Holy Spirit,
one God, for ever and ever. Amen.

AFFIRMATION OF FAITH

Based on John 3:5–6, 14–17

What do we believe concerning the kingdom of God and eternal life?

We believe that no one can enter the kingdom of God without being born of water and Spirit.
What is born of the flesh is flesh, and what is born of the Spirit is spirit.
We believe that as Moses lifted up the serpent in the wilderness, so the Son of Man was lifted up—that whoever believes in him may have eternal life.
We believe that God so loved the world that he gave his only Son, so that everyone who believes in him may not perish but may have eternal life. Indeed, God did not send the Son into the world to condemn the world, but in order that the world might be saved through him.

Proper 3 (Year B)

Sunday between May 24 and May 28 inclusive

LECTIONARY READINGS

Hosea 2:14–20
Psalm 103:1–13, 22
2 Corinthians 3:1–6
Mark 2:13–22

CALL TO WORSHIP

Psalm 103:11–13

For as the heavens are high above the earth,
so great is his steadfast love toward those who fear him;
as far as the east is from the west,
so far he removes our transgressions from us.
**As a father has compassion for his children,
so the Lord has compassion for those who fear him.**

PRAYER OF RENEWAL

Based on Mark 2:13–17

Lord Jesus,
you call us to follow you;
to lay aside our own agendas and seek your kingdom.
Like Levi, we want to find ourselves
surrounded by others who have sought
and found your grace and forgiveness.
Help us to come as we are, but not stay as we are.
Transform us and give us a heart for this broken world,
reaching out in love to those who need your grace and mercy.
In the name of Jesus we pray. Amen.

AFFIRMATION OF FAITH

Based on 2 Corinthians 3:3

What do we believe concerning our testimony to the world?

We believe that we are a letter of Christ, written not with ink
but with the Spirit of the living God,
not on tablets of stone but on tablets of human hearts.

Proper 4 (Year B)

Sunday between May 29 and June 4 inclusive

LECTIONARY READINGS

Deuteronomy 5:12–15
Psalm 81:1–10
2 Corinthians 4:5–12
Mark 2:23–3:6

CALL TO WORSHIP

Psalm 81:1–2

Sing aloud to God our strength;
shout for joy to the God of Jacob.
Raise a song, sound the tambourine,
the sweet lyre with the harp.

PRAYER OF RENEWAL

Based on Deuteronomy 5:12–14; 2 Corinthians 4:7–11

Holy God,
you have woven into our very being
the rhythm of one day in seven for rest, for sabbath.
May we see this as a life-giving ordinance
for worship and for the renewal of our souls.
Give us strength, for we are only fragile jars of clay.
Remind us that all power comes from you and not ourselves.
Though we face trials and afflictions, we are not crushed;
though we may feel confused and perplexed, we do not despair;
though we may experience persecution, you are always with us.
Help us put to death all that is not pleasing to you,
so that the life of Christ may become more and more evident in us. Amen.

AFFIRMATION OF FAITH

Based on Deuteronomy 5:12–14; Mark 2:27–28; 3:4–5

What do we believe concerning the Sabbath?

We believe God created a rhythm in creation—
one day in seven for sabbath rest.
We believe the Sabbath was made for humankind,
and not humankind for the Sabbath.
We further affirm that the Son of Man is Lord even of the Sabbath.
We believe the sabbath brings us opportunities
to do good and not harm; to bring life, not destroy it.

Proper 5 (Year B)

Sunday between June 5 and June 11 inclusive

LECTIONARY READINGS

Genesis 3:8–15
Psalm 130
2 Corinthians 4:13–5:1
Mark 3:20–35

CALL TO WORSHIP

Psalm 130:1–2, 5–6

Out of the depths I cry to you, O Lord. Lord, hear my voice!
Let your ears be attentive to the voice of my supplications!
I wait for the Lord, my soul waits, and in his word I hope;
my soul waits for the Lord
more than those who watch for the morning,
more than those who watch for the morning.

PRAYER OF RENEWAL

Based on Genesis 3:8–12

Merciful God,
when we hide ourselves in shame, you seek us out in love.
We ask for the courage to tell you truthfully how we have sinned,
and how we have been sinned against.
Help us not to place blame on others, but to confess our own shortcomings.
We pray for forgiveness so that we can live at peace
with ourselves, with others, and with you.
You alone can restore us.
In steadfast love, look upon us and reclothe us in your grace;
through Jesus Christ our Lord. Amen.

AFFIRMATION OF FAITH

Based on 2 Corinthians 4:14, 16–18

What do we believe concerning our eternal glory?

We believe that the one who raised the Lord Jesus will raise us also with Jesus, and will bring us, with all the saints, into his presence.
We do not lose heart, for we believe that even though our outer nature is wasting away, our inner nature is being renewed day by day.
We believe that this slight momentary affliction is preparing us for an eternal weight of glory beyond all measure, because we look not at what can be seen but at what cannot be seen;
for what can be seen is temporary, but what cannot be seen is eternal.

Proper 6 (Year B)

Sunday between June 12 and June 18 inclusive

LECTIONARY READINGS

Ezekiel 17:22–24
Psalm 92:1–4, 12–15
2 Corinthians 5:6–17
Mark 4:26–34

CALL TO WORSHIP

Psalm 92:1–4

It is good to give thanks to the Lord,
to sing praises to your name, O Most High;
to declare your steadfast love in the morning, and your faithfulness by night,
to the music of the lute and the harp, to the melody of the lyre.
For you, O Lord, have made me glad by your work;
at the works of your hands I sing for joy.

PRAYER OF INTERCESSION

Based on Mark 4:26–27; 2 Corinthians 5:17

Lord Jesus, as your people, we are a new creation.
Help us to live out this new life in our relationships with you,
with ourselves, and with one another.
Edify and strengthen us in word and in deed.
Give us bold faith to play our part in scattering seed;
then watching with expectancy for the power of your Spirit
at work, night and day, to bring growth and vitality.
Bring about justice and peace and make our schools, workplaces,
and our homes safe for all to thrive.
Tear down walls of hostility and prejudice.

We pray for those in need:
for those in financial difficulty, we ask for provision;
for those with physical ailments, we ask for healing and comfort;
for those battling addictions, we pray for honesty and disclosure;
for those in the darkness of depression, we ask for rays of hope;
for those who have lost loved ones, we ask for your abiding presence and peace. In the name of the Father, the Son, and the Holy Spirit. Amen.

AFFIRMATION OF FAITH

Based on 2 Corinthians 5:17

What do we believe concerning our new creation in Christ?

We believe that if anyone is in Christ, he is a new creation:
everything old has passed away; everything has become new.

Proper 7 (Year B)

Sunday between June 19 and June 25 inclusive

LECTIONARY READINGS

Job 38:1–11
Psalm 107:1–3, 23–32
2 Corinthians 6:1–13
Mark 4:35–41

CALL TO WORSHIP

Psalm 107:1–3

O give thanks to the Lord, for he is good; for his steadfast love endures forever.
**Let the redeemed of the Lord say so, those he redeemed from trouble
and gathered in from the lands, from the east and from the west,
from the north and from the south.**

PRAYER OF RENEWAL

Based on Mark 4:37–41; Job 38:4, 8–11

Lord Jesus,
we confess that when the storms of life come our way,
we are often full of fear rather than faith.
Though you laid the earth's foundations
and gave the sea its boundaries,
we question your presence and power in our lives.
Help us to trust in your care over all creation
and the circumstances of our everyday lives.
Speak peace and stillness to our troubled hearts.
In the powerful name of Jesus we pray. Amen.

AFFIRMATION OF FAITH

Based on 2 Corinthians 6:3–8

How were the apostles commended for the service to God?

We believe they were commended in every way: through great endurance, in afflictions, hardships, calamities, beatings, imprisonments, riots, labors, sleepless nights, hunger; by purity, knowledge, patience, kindness, holiness of spirit, genuine love, truthful speech, and the power of God; with the weapons of righteousness for the right hand and for the left; in honor and dishonor, in ill repute and good repute.

Proper 8 (Year B)

Sunday between June 26 and July 2 inclusive

LECTIONARY READINGS

Lamentations 3:22–33
Psalm 30
2 Corinthians 8:7–15
Mark 5:21–43

CALL TO WORSHIP

Lamentations 3:22–24

The steadfast love of the Lord never ceases,
his mercies never come to an end;
they are new every morning; great is your faithfulness.
"The Lord is my portion," says my soul, "therefore I will hope in him."

PRAYER OF RENEWAL

Based on Mark 5:21–43; 2 Corinthians 8:7–15

Lord Jesus,
we know you are a generous and healing God,
sustaining us and providing for us in so many ways.
We acknowledge our various forms of sickness and suffering.
We battle addictions, disease, and depression.
Give us faith in your power to make us well
and courage to walk the path you have for us.
We confess that too often we lack a spirit of generosity,
wanting to hold on to what we have,
falsely thinking your gifts are ours to keep.
Fill us with an eagerness to give, a desire to meet others' needs,
and a joy in sharing for the glory of your kingdom.

Forgive us, heal us, and make us new
through the grace and mercy of Christ. Amen.

AFFIRMATION OF FAITH

Based on 2 Corinthians 8:9

What do we believe concerning the generosity of our Lord?

We believe in the generous act of our Lord Jesus Christ,
that though he was rich,
yet for our sake he became poor,
so that by his poverty we might become rich.

Proper 9 (Year B)

Sunday between July 3 and July 9 inclusive

LECTIONARY READINGS

Ezekiel 2:1–5
Psalm 123
2 Corinthians 12:2–10
Mark 6:1–13

CALL TO WORSHIP

Psalm 123:1–2

To you I lift up my eyes, O you who are enthroned in the heavens!
As the eyes of servants look to the hand of their master, as the eyes of a maid to the hand of her mistress, so our eyes look to the Lord our God, until he has mercy upon us.

PRAYER OF RENEWAL

Based on Ezekiel 2:1–5; Mark 6:1–5; 2 Corinthians 12:10

Lord Jesus, we confess that we can be
a rebellious and stubborn people.
With our mouths we profess you as Lord,
but in our lives we harbor disbelief,
doubting your wisdom, power, and mighty deeds.
Take away our hardness of heart, and fill us with childlike faith
in your prophetic word and comforting presence.
Grant us contentment in all that comes our way:
weaknesses, insults, hardships, persecutions, and calamities;
for when we are weak, then we are strong.
In Christ's name we pray. Amen.

AFFIRMATION OF FAITH

Based on Mark 6:7–8, 12–13

What do we believe concerning the Lord's sending of the disciples?

We believe that Jesus called the twelve disciples and sent them out two by two, giving them authority over the unclean spirits.
We believe that Jesus ordered them to take nothing for their journey except a staff; no bread, no bag, no money in their belts.
We believe they went out and proclaimed that all should repent. They cast out many demons, and anointed with oil many who were sick and cured them.

Proper 10 (Year B)

Sunday between July 10 and July 16 inclusive

LECTIONARY READINGS

Amos 7:7–15
Psalm 85:8–13
Ephesians 1:3–14
Mark 6:14–29

CALL TO WORSHIP

Psalm 85:8–9

Let us hear what God the Lord will speak,
for he will speak peace to his people, to his faithful,
to those who turn to him in their hearts.
**Surely his salvation is at hand for those who fear him,
that his glory may dwell in our land.**

PRAYER OF RENEWAL

Based on Mark 6:14–29

Lord God, we confess that, at times, we hold grudges toward others.
Because of the sinfulness in our hearts, our words and actions
can hurt family members, neighbors, friends, and co-workers.
Open our eyes to see the resentments we carry inside.
Help us to find forgiveness so that our hearts and minds may be set free
from evil thoughts that burden our soul and squelch our intimacy with you.
In Christ's name we pray. Amen.

AFFIRMATION OF FAITH

Based on Ephesians 1:3–8

What do we believe concerning our spiritual blessings in Christ?

We believe that the God and Father of our Lord Jesus Christ
has blessed us in Christ with every spiritual blessing in the heavenly places,
just as he chose us in Christ before the foundation of the world
to be holy and blameless before him in love.
We believe that he predestined us for adoption as his children through Jesus Christ,
according to the good pleasure of his will, to the praise of his glorious grace that he freely bestowed on us in the Beloved.
We believe that in Christ we have redemption through his blood, the forgiveness of our trespasses, according to the riches of his grace that he lavished on us.

Proper 11 (Year B)

Sunday between July 17 and July 23 inclusive

LECTIONARY READINGS

Jeremiah 23:1–6
Psalm 23
Ephesians 2:11–22
Mark 6:30–34, 53–56

CALL TO WORSHIP

Based on Mark 6:31, Psalm 23:1–3

As Jesus called the apostles to a place of rest,
so, too, does our Good Shepherd call us
to walk beside the still waters of worship,
restoring our souls and leading us in right paths for his name's sake.
Let us worship the Lord.

PRAYER OF RENEWAL

Based on Psalm 23

Jesus, our Good Shepherd,
in you we have all that we truly desire.
Guide us to green pastures and lead us beside still waters.
Where our souls lack health, bring restoration.
Lead us in right paths that you may be glorified.
When we walk through dark times,
remove our fears and fill us with faith.
Remind us of your Spirit's presence to comfort and guide us.
Help us to love our enemies and remember
your goodness and mercy at the close of each day.
In Christ's name we pray. Amen.

AFFIRMATION OF FAITH

Based on Ephesians 2:13, 19–20

What do we believe concerning our membership in the household of God?

We believe that we, who once were far off, have been brought near by the blood of Christ.
We believe we are no longer strangers and aliens, but we are citizens with the saints and also members of the household of God, built upon the foundation of the apostles and prophets, with Christ Jesus himself as the cornerstone.

Proper 12 (Year B)

Sunday between July 24 and July 30 inclusive

LECTIONARY READINGS

2 Kings 4:42–44
Psalm 145:10–18
Ephesians 3:14–21
John 6:1–21

CALL TO WORSHIP

Psalm 145:10–12

All your works shall give thanks to you, O Lord,
and all your faithful shall bless you.
They shall speak of the glory of your kingdom, and tell of your power, to make known to all people your mighty deeds, and the glorious splendor of your kingdom.

PRAYER OF RENEWAL

Based on Ephesians 3:14–21

Father, we pray, according to the riches of your glory,
that we may be strengthened in our inner being
with power through your Spirit,
and that Christ may dwell in our hearts through faith,
as we are being rooted and grounded in love.
We pray that we may have the power to comprehend,
with all the saints, what is the breadth and length and height and depth,
and to know the love of Christ that surpasses knowledge,
so that we may be filled with all the fullness of God.
Now to him who by the power at work within us
is able to accomplish abundantly far more than all we can ask or imagine,

to him be glory in the church and in Christ Jesus
to all generations, forever and ever. Amen.

AFFIRMATION OF FAITH

Based on Psalm 145:13b–18

What do we believe concerning the character of God?

We believe the Lord is faithful in all his words, and gracious in all his deeds.
We believe the Lord upholds all who are falling, and raises up all who are bowed down.
We believe the eyes of all look to the Lord, and he gives them their food in due season.
We believe the Lord opens his hand, satisfying the desire of every living thing.
We believe the Lord is just in all his ways, and kind in all his doings.
We believe the Lord is near to all who call on him, to all who call on him in truth.

Proper 13 (Year B)

Sunday between July 31 and August 6 inclusive

LECTIONARY READINGS

Exodus 16:2–4, 9–15
Psalm 78:23–29
Ephesians 4:1–16
John 6:24–35

CALL TO WORSHIP

Based on Psalm 78:23, 29

Our God commands the skies above, and opens the doors of heaven.
He provides food to satisfy our deepest cravings.
As we come to you in worship, O Lord, may you fill our hungry and thirsty souls.

PRAYER OF RENEWAL

Based on Exodus 16:2–3; John 6:27, 33, 35

Rescuing God, we confess that we quickly forget
your faithfulness and redemption in our lives.
Like the Israelites we romance our days in bondage
and complain about your lack of provision in our lives.
Though you call us to yourself to fill our deepest hunger and thirst,
we run back to food that does not satisfy.
Bread of life, may we not strive for the food that perishes,
but for food that endures for eternal life.
You are the source of life to the world, help us to rest in you alone.
In Christ's name we pray. Amen.

AFFIRMATION OF FAITH

Based on Ephesians 4:4–7, 11–13

What do we believe concerning the body and the Spirit, the hope of our calling, and the gifts of Christ?

We believe there is one body and one Spirit, just as we were called to the one hope of our calling—one Lord, one faith, one baptism, one God and Father of all, who is above all and through all and in all.
We believe that when Christ ascended to heaven, he gave gifts to his people. The gifts he gave were that some would be apostles, some prophets, some evangelists, some pastors and teachers, to equip the saints for the work of ministry, for building up the body of Christ, until all of us come to the unity of the faith and of the knowledge of the Son of God, to maturity, to the measure of the full stature of Christ.

Proper 14 (Year B)

Sunday between August 7 and August 13 inclusive

LECTIONARY READINGS

1 Kings 19:4–8
Psalm 34:1–8
Ephesians 4:25–5:2
John 6:35, 41–51

CALL TO WORSHIP

Psalm 34:1–3

I will bless the Lord at all times;
his praise shall continually be in my mouth.
My soul makes its boast in the Lord;
let the humble hear and be glad.
O magnify the Lord with me,
and let us exalt his name together.

PRAYER OF RENEWAL

Based on Psalm 34:4–8; John 6:47–51

Restoring God,
you are the one who answers our prayers
and delivers us from all our fears.
We look to you and are radiant;
in you there is no shame or condemnation.
You are the bread of life, who came down from heaven,
and who brings eternal life to those who believe.
Help us to worship and follow you this day,
to taste and see that you are good.
We are blessed when we take refuge in you. Amen.

AFFIRMATION OF FAITH

Based on Ephesians 4:31–5:2

How are we to live as followers of Christ?

We believe we are to put away all bitterness and wrath
and anger and wrangling and slander, together with all malice, and be kind to one another,
tenderhearted, forgiving one another, as God in Christ has forgiven us.
We believe we are to be imitators of God, as beloved children, and live in love, as Christ loved us and gave himself up for us, a fragrant offering and sacrifice to God.

Proper 15 (Year B)

Sunday between August 14 and August 20 inclusive

LECTIONARY READINGS

Proverbs 9:1–6
Psalm 34:9–14
Ephesians 5:15–20
John 6:51–58

CALL TO WORSHIP

Based on Ephesians 5:18–20

Brothers and sisters, may we be filled with the Spirit,
as we sing psalms and hymns and spiritual songs together.
We come singing and making melody to the Lord in our hearts,
giving thanks to God the Father in the name of our Lord Jesus Christ.

PRAYER OF RENEWAL

Based on Proverbs 9:3–6; John 6:51; Ephesians 5:15–20

Holy God,
we confess that we do not always heed wisdom's call:
we do not lay aside immaturity, nor walk in the way of insight.
We are not careful about how we live,
making the most of our time because this world is full of evil.
We do not nourish ourselves with the bread of life,
but foolishly seek temporary satisfaction in wine and sensual pleasures.
God, our Father, forgive us and help us to abide in you.
Fill us with your Holy Spirit and may we give you thanks
at all times and for everything in the name of our Lord Jesus Christ;
in whose name we pray. Amen.

AFFIRMATION OF FAITH

Based on Ephesians 5:15–16, 18–20

How are we to live as wise followers of Christ?

We believe we are to be careful about how we live,
not as unwise people but as wise, making the most of the time, because the days are evil.
We believe we should not get drunk with wine, for that is debauchery;
but be filled with the Spirit, as we sing psalms and hymns and spiritual songs among ourselves, singing and making melody to the Lord in our hearts, giving thanks to God the Father at all times and for everything in the name of our Lord Jesus Christ.

Proper 16 (Year B)

Sunday between August 21 and August 27 inclusive

LECTIONARY READINGS

Joshua 24:1–2a, 14–18
Psalm 34:15–22
Ephesians 6:10–20
John 6:56–69

CALL TO WORSHIP

Based on Joshua 24:15–18

Choose this day whom you will serve.
It is the Lord our God who brought us up from the land of Egypt, out of the house of slavery, and who did great signs in our sight. He protected us along all the way that we went, and among all the peoples through whom we passed. Therefore we will serve the Lord, for he is our God.

PRAYER OF RENEWAL

Based on Psalm 34:15–20

Gracious God,
we know your eyes are on your children,
and that your ears are open to our cries.
When we call on you for help you hear us, and rescue us from all our troubles.
We praise you, for you are near to the brokenhearted, and save the crushed in spirit.
Many are the afflictions of your people, but you rescue us from them all.
You redeem the life of your servants; none who take refuge in you will be condemned. In the name of Jesus we pray. Amen.

AFFIRMATION OF FAITH

Based on Ephesians 6:10–18

What do we believe concerning our struggle against evil and the armor of God?

We believe our struggle is not against enemies of flesh and blood, but against the rulers, against the authorities, against the cosmic powers of this present darkness, against the spiritual forces of evil in the heavenly places.
Therefore, we believe that we are to take up the whole armor of God, so that we may be able to stand firm: the belt of truth around our waist, and the breastplate of righteousness; shoes for our feet that will make us ready to proclaim the gospel of peace; the shield of faith, with which we will be able to quench all the flaming arrows of the evil one; the helmet of salvation, and the sword of the Spirit, which is the word of God.

Proper 17 (Year B)

Sunday between August 28 and September 3 inclusive

LECTIONARY READINGS

Deuteronomy 4:1–2, 6–9
Psalm 15
James 1:17–27
Mark 7:1–8, 14–15, 21–23

CALL TO WORSHIP

Based on Mark 7:6–7

Brothers and sisters, may we not be like hypocrites
who honor God with their lips, but whose hearts are far from him.
May we not worship in vain, but in spirit and in truth.

PRAYER OF RENEWAL

Based on Psalm 15

O Lord, we long to abide and dwell with you.
Help us to walk blamelessly, to do what is right,
and to speak the truth from our heart.
Keep us from slandering others with our tongue,
from harming our friends, and from criticizing our neighbors.
God of all grace, may we despise evil acts,
and honor those who fear the Lord;
Give us the strength to keep our promises even when it hurts.
May we not lend money with interest,
nor take a bribe against the innocent.
Help us in all these ways, O Lord, that we may stand firm forever. Amen.

AFFIRMATION OF FAITH

Based on James 1:19, 22, 27

How are we to act as followers of Christ?

We believe we are to be quick to listen, slow to speak, slow to anger;
for our anger does not produce God's righteousness.
We believe we are to be doers of the word, and not merely hearers who deceive themselves.

What do we believe concerning religion that is pure and undefiled before God?

We believe that religion that is pure and undefiled before God, the Father, is this: to care for orphans and widows in their distress,
and to keep oneself unstained by the world.

Proper 18 (Year B)

Sunday between September 4 and September 10 inclusive

LECTIONARY READINGS

Isaiah 35:4–7
Psalm 146
James 2:1–17
Mark 7:24–37

CALL TO WORSHIP

Psalm 146:1–2

Praise the Lord! Praise the Lord, O my soul!
I will praise the Lord as long as I live;
I will sing praises to my God all my life long.

PRAYER OF INTERCESSION

Based on Isaiah 35:4–7, Mark 7:34–35

Mighty God,
you urge us to be strong and not to fear, for you will come to save us.
So we pray boldly for your kingdom to come on earth as it is in heaven.
From your healing touch may the eyes of the blind be opened,
and the ears of the deaf unstopped.
May the feet of the lame leap like a deer,
and the tongue of the speechless sing for joy.
From your redeeming love may
waters break forth in the wilderness, and streams in the desert.
May the burning sand become a pool, and the thirsty ground springs of water.
With just a word, you are able to heal us, redeem us, and make all things new;
through Jesus Christ our Lord. Amen.

AFFIRMATION OF FAITH

Based on James 2:8, 12–13, 17

What do we believe concerning love of neighbor, judgment and mercy, faith and works?

We believe we are to fulfill the law according to the scripture,
"You shall love your neighbor as yourself."
We believe we are to speak and to act as those who are to be judged by the law of liberty.
For we believe that judgment will be without mercy to anyone who has shown no mercy.
We believe that mercy triumphs over judgment.
We believe that faith by itself, if it has no works, is dead.

Proper 19 (Year B)

Sunday between September 11 and September 17 inclusive

LECTIONARY READINGS

Isaiah 50:4–9a
Psalm 116:1–9
James 3:1–12
Mark 8:27–38

CALL TO WORSHIP

Psalm 116:5–7

Gracious is the Lord, and righteous; our God is merciful.
The Lord protects the simple; when I was brought low, he saved me.
Return, O my soul, to your rest,
for the Lord has dealt bountifully with you.

PRAYER OF RENEWAL

Based on James 3:5–10, Isaiah 50:4

Lord, we confess that our tongue
can be used for evil and is full of deadly poison.
It is like a fire that can set a forest ablaze.
With it we bless the Lord, but also curse
those who are made in the likeness of God.
From the same mouth come blessing and cursing.
Merciful God, give us tongues that are able
to sustain the weary with just a word.
Let our mouths be used to edify and encourage,
rather than tear down and destroy;
through Jesus Christ our Lord. Amen.

AFFIRMATION OF FAITH

Based on Mark 8:29, 31, 34–35

What do we believe concerning Jesus, his life, and our lives as his disciples?

We believe that Jesus is the Messiah.
We believe that the Son of Man endured great suffering; was rejected by the elders,
the chief priests, and the scribes; was killed, and after three days rose again.
We believe that all who want to become disciples of Christ must deny themselves, take up their cross and follow him. For those who want to save their life will lose it, and those who lose their life for Christ's sake, and for the sake of the gospel, will save it.

Proper 20 (Year B)

Sunday between September 18 and September 24 inclusive

LECTIONARY READINGS

Jeremiah 11:18–20
Psalm 54
James 3:13–4:3, 7–8a
Mark 9:30–37

CALL TO WORSHIP

Psalm 54:6

With a freewill offering I will sacrifice to you;
I will give thanks to your name, O Lord, for it is good.

PRAYER OF RENEWAL

Based on Mark 9:34–37

Gracious God, you told the disciples that whoever wants
to be first must be last of all and servant of all.
We confess that we are often driven
by selfish ambition and a desire to be the greatest.
Grant us a humility of heart that, in your name,
we would welcome the children among us,
the least among us, the broken among us.
Help us to serve others rather than ourselves;
through Jesus Christ, our Savior and Lord. Amen.

AFFIRMATION OF FAITH

Based on James 3:16–18; 4:7–8

What do we believe concerning ambition, wisdom, and submission to God?

We believe that where there is envy and selfish ambition,
there will also be disorder and wickedness of every kind.
We believe that the wisdom from above is first pure, then peaceable, gentle,
willing to yield, full of mercy and good fruits, without a trace of partiality
or hypocrisy.
We believe that a harvest of righteousness is sown in peace for those who
make peace.
We believe that we are to submit ourselves to God.
We believe that if we resist the devil, he will flee from us;
and that when we draw near to God, he will draw near to us.

Proper 21 (Year B)

Sunday between September 25 and October 1 inclusive

LECTIONARY READINGS

Numbers 11:4–6, 10–16, 24–29
Psalm 19:7–14
James 5:13–20
Mark 9:38–50

CALL TO WORSHIP

Based on Psalm 19:14

Lord Jesus, as we gather together in worship,
let the words of our mouths and the meditations of our hearts
be acceptable to you, our rock and our redeemer.

PRAYER OF INTERCESSION

Based on James 5:13–20

God of healing and grace,
we come with intercessions for those among us:
For those who are suffering, we lift up our prayers.
For those who are cheerful, we join in their songs of praise.
For those who are sick, we ask for your anointing power and healing touch.
Fill us all with faith, like Elijah, as we pray for one another
and confess our sins to one another, that we may be healed.
Use us to bring back those who have wandered from the truth;
may their souls be saved from death; may their sins be covered by your grace.
In the name of Jesus we pray. Amen.

AFFIRMATION OF FAITH

Based on Psalm 19:7–10

What do we believe concerning the law and commandments of the Lord?

We believe the law of the Lord is perfect, reviving the soul;
and the decrees of the Lord are sure, making wise the simple;
We believe the precepts of the Lord are right, rejoicing the heart;
and the commandments of the Lord are clear, enlightening the eyes.
We believe the fear of the Lord is pure, enduring forever;
and the ordinances of the Lord are true and righteous altogether.
We believe the ordinances of the Lord are to be desired more than gold, even much fine gold.
We believe they are sweeter also than honey, and drippings of the honeycomb.

Proper 22 (Year B)

Sunday between October 2 and October 8 inclusive

LECTIONARY READINGS

Genesis 2:18–24
Psalm 8
Hebrews 1:1–4; 2:5–12
Mark 10:2–16

CALL TO WORSHIP

Psalm 8:1–2

O Lord, our Sovereign, how majestic is your name in all the earth!
You have set your glory above the heavens.

PRAYER OF RENEWAL

Based on Genesis 2:18–24

Creator God,
we know it is not good for humankind to be alone.
We thank you for the covenant of marriage
and the intimacy between husband and wife.
Give us the grace, in all of our relationships,
to love and serve one another with the love of Christ.
We thank you for the gift of creation,
animals of the field and birds of the air.
May we be good stewards of the earth,
exercising care and dominion over all that you have made;
through Jesus Christ our Lord. Amen.

AFFIRMATION OF FAITH

Based on Hebrews 1:1–4

What do we believe concerning the revelation of God and the ministry of Jesus?

We believe that long ago God spoke to his people in many and various ways by the prophets,
but in these last days he has spoken to us by his Son, Jesus, whom he appointed heir of all things, through whom he also created the worlds.
We believe Jesus is the reflection of God's glory and the exact imprint of God's very being, and that he sustains all things by his powerful word.
We believe that when Jesus had made purification for sins, he sat down at the right hand of the Majesty on high, having become as much superior to angels as the name he has inherited is more excellent than theirs.

Proper 23 (Year B)

Sunday between October 9 and October 15 inclusive

LECTIONARY READINGS

Amos 5:6–7, 10–15
Psalm 90:12–17
Hebrews 4:12–16
Mark 10:17–31

CALL TO WORSHIP

Psalm 90:14

Satisfy us in the morning with your steadfast love,
so that we may rejoice and be glad all our days.

PRAYER OF RENEWAL

Based on Amos 5:14–15

Merciful God,
help us to seek good and not evil, that we may live;
and so that you, O Lord, will be with us.
Establish justice in our hearts and in our communities.
Be gracious to us and smile upon us with your favor;
through Jesus Christ our Lord. Amen.

AFFIRMATION OF FAITH

Based on Hebrews 4:12–16

What do we believe concerning the word of God and the priestly ministry of Christ?

We believe the word of God is living and active,
sharper than any two-edged sword, piercing until it divides soul from spirit, joints from marrow; able to judge the thoughts and intentions of the heart.
We believe we have a great high priest
who has passed through the heavens, Jesus, the Son of God.
We believe our high priest is able to sympathize with our weaknesses;
for he has, in every respect, been tested as we are, yet without sin.
We believe, therefore, that we can approach the throne of grace with boldness, so that we may receive mercy and find grace to help in time of need.

Proper 24 (Year B)

Sunday between October 16 and October 22 inclusive

LECTIONARY READINGS

Isaiah 53:4–12
Psalm 91:9–16
Hebrews 5:1–10
Mark 10:35–45

CALL TO WORSHIP

Psalm 91:14–16

Those who love me, I will deliver; I will protect those who know my name.
When they call to me, I will answer them;
I will be with them in trouble, I will rescue them and honor them.
With long life I will satisfy them, and show them my salvation.

PRAYER OF RENEWAL

Based on Mark 10:35–45

Gracious Lord,
we confess that we desire positions
of power and authority and to make a name for ourselves.
Change our hearts, O God; give us the humility of Christ,
who came not to be served but to serve.
May we remember that whoever wishes
to become great must become a servant,
and whoever wishes to be first must be slave of all.
In the name of Jesus we pray. Amen.

AFFIRMATION OF FAITH

Based on Hebrews 5:7–10

What do we believe concerning the prayers and obedience of Christ?

We believe that in the days that Jesus walked the earth, he offered up prayers and supplications, with loud cries and tears, to the one who was able to save him from death,
and he was heard because of his reverent submission.
We believe that although he was a Son, he learned obedience through what he suffered;
and having been made perfect, he became the source of eternal salvation for all who obey him, having been designated by God a high priest.

Proper 25 (Year B)

Sunday between October 23 and October 29 inclusive

LECTIONARY READINGS

Jeremiah 31:7–9
Psalm 126
Hebrews 7:23–28
Mark 10:46–52

CALL TO WORSHIP

Jeremiah 31:7

For thus says the Lord: Sing aloud with gladness for Jacob,
and raise shouts for the chief of the nations; proclaim, give praise, and say,
"Save, O Lord, your people, the remnant of Israel."

PRAYER OF INTERCESSION

Based on Psalm 126; Mark 10:46–52

Gracious Lord, we can look back and see
your hand of faithfulness in our lives; seasons of redemption and restoration,
when our mouths were filled with laughter, and our tongues with shouts of
joy. You have done have great things for us, and we have rejoiced.
Restore our hearts and our health once again, O Lord,
like streams in the desert.
May those who sow in tears reap with shouts of joy.
May those who go out weeping, bearing the seed for sowing,
come home with shouts of joy, carrying the fruit of your hand.
In the name of Jesus we pray. Amen.

AFFIRMATION OF FAITH

Based on Hebrews 7:23–25, 27

What do we believe concerning the priesthood of Christ?

We believe that Jesus holds his priesthood permanently,
because he continues forever.
We believe that he is able for all time to save those
who approach God through him,
since he always lives to make intercession for them.
We believe that, unlike the other high priests,
Jesus has no need to offer sacrifices day after day,
first for his own sins, and then for those of the people;
this he did once for all when he offered himself.

Proper 26 (Year B)

Sunday between October 30 and November 5 inclusive

LECTIONARY READINGS

Deuteronomy 6:1–9
Psalm 119:1–8
Hebrews 9:11–14
Mark 12:28–34

CALL TO WORSHIP

Psalm 119:5–7

O that my ways may be steadfast
in keeping your statutes!
Then I shall not be put to shame,
having my eyes fixed on all your commandments.
I will praise you with an upright heart,
when I learn your righteous ordinances.

PRAYER OF RENEWAL

Based on Psalm 119:1–7

Triune God,
we know that those who walk in the law of the Lord,
and whose way is blameless, have peace in their hearts.
We confess that our souls are not at rest.
We are disturbed and downcast for we do need keep your word.
We do not walk with you as we should; nor love you with our whole heart;
we are not steadfast in keeping your commands.
Help us to keep our eyes fixed on all your ways,
and to praise you with an upright heart.

We desire rest for our souls;
we want to be satisfied in you alone. Amen.

AFFIRMATION OF FAITH

Based on Mark 12:30–31

What do we believe concerning the two greatest commandments?

We believe that we are to love the Lord our God with all our heart,
and with all our soul, and with all our mind, and with all our strength.
We believe we are to love our neighbor as ourself.
We believe that there is no other commandment greater than these.

Proper 27 (Year B)

Sunday between November 6 and November 12 inclusive

LECTIONARY READINGS

1 Kings 17:8–16
Psalm 146
Hebrews 9:24–28
Mark 12:38–44

CALL TO WORSHIP

Psalm 146:1–2

Praise the Lord! Praise the Lord, O my soul!
I will praise the Lord as long as I live;
I will sing praises to my God all my life long.

PRAYER OF RENEWAL

Based on 1 Kings 17:8–16; Mark 12:38–44

Sovereign Lord,
we know that your word comes to us,
and that your Holy Spirit guides us
in the ordinary events of life.
Often, when it seems our resources have been depleted,
you provide for us and sustain us in amazing ways.
You care for us like the widow in Zarephath,
whose jar of meal was not emptied,
and whose jug of oil did not fail.
O Lord, may we not walk around pridefully,
desiring approval and places of honor in this world.

Rather, from a poverty in spirit, may we find abundance;
from a heart of gratitude, may we offer you all that we have.
In the name of Jesus we pray. Amen.

AFFIRMATION OF FAITH

Based on Hebrews 9:24, 26, 28

What do we believe concerning Christ's presence in heaven, his sacrifice, and his return?

We believe that Christ entered into heaven itself,
to appear in the presence of God on our behalf.
We believe Christ has appeared once for all to remove sin by the sacrifice of himself.
We believe that Christ, having been offered once to bear the sins of many, will appear a second time, not to deal with sin,
but to save those who are eagerly waiting for him.

Proper 28 (Year B)

Sunday between November 13 and November 19 inclusive

LECTIONARY READINGS

Daniel 12:1–3
Psalm 16
Hebrews 10:11–25
Mark 13:1–8

CALL TO WORSHIP

Based on Hebrews 10:22–25

Let us come to worship with a true heart in full assurance of faith,
with our hearts sprinkled clean from an evil conscience and our bodies washed with pure water.
Let us hold fast to the confession of our hope without wavering,
for he who has promised is faithful.
And let us consider how to provoke one another to love and good deeds,
not neglecting to meet together, as is the habit of some,
but encouraging one another, and all the more as we see the Day approaching.

PRAYER OF RENEWAL

Based on Psalm 16:1–2, 6–9, 11

Lord Jesus,
in you we take refuge.
You are our Lord; we have no good apart from you.
In your grace and mercy, the boundary lines
have fallen for us in pleasant places;
we have a godly heritage.
Through the Spirit, you give us counsel and guidance.
We know that you are always with us; we will not be moved.

Our hearts are glad and our souls rejoice for you show us the path of life.
In your presence there is fullness of joy;
in your right hand are pleasures forevermore. Amen.

AFFIRMATION OF FAITH

Based on Daniel 12:1

What do we believe concerning the last days?

We believe that in the last days there will be a time of anguish,
such as has never occurred since nations first came into existence.
We believe that God's people shall be delivered,
everyone who is found written in the book.

Christ the King (Year B)

LECTIONARY READINGS

Daniel 7:9–10, 13–14
Psalm 93
Revelation 1:4b–8
John 18:33–37

CALL TO WORSHIP

Psalm 93:1–2

The Lord is king, he is robed in majesty;
the Lord is robed, he is girded with strength.
He has established the world; it shall never be moved;
your throne is established from of old; you are from everlasting.

PRAYER OF RENEWAL

Based on John 18:33–37

Lord Jesus,
we confess that, like Pilate,
we sometimes question your kingship.
Too often, we desire to rule and manage our own lives.
Help us submit to your will and your authority,
for you love us, care for us, and know what is best for us.
Remind us that your kingdom is not of this world,
and that your ways are not our ways.
Help us to listen to your voice,
and grant us an undivided heart, wholly devoted to you.
In the name of Jesus we pray. Amen.

AFFIRMATION OF FAITH

Based on Daniel 7:13–14; Revelation 1:7–8

What do we believe concerning the reign and return of Jesus?

We believe that when Jesus returns he will be coming
with the clouds of heaven, and every eye will see him.
We believe he was given dominion and glory and kingship,
that all peoples, nations, and languages should serve him.
We believe that his dominion is an everlasting dominion
that shall not pass away, and his kingship is one that shall never be destroyed.
We believe Jesus is the Alpha and the Omega, who is and who was and who
is to come.

The Year of Luke

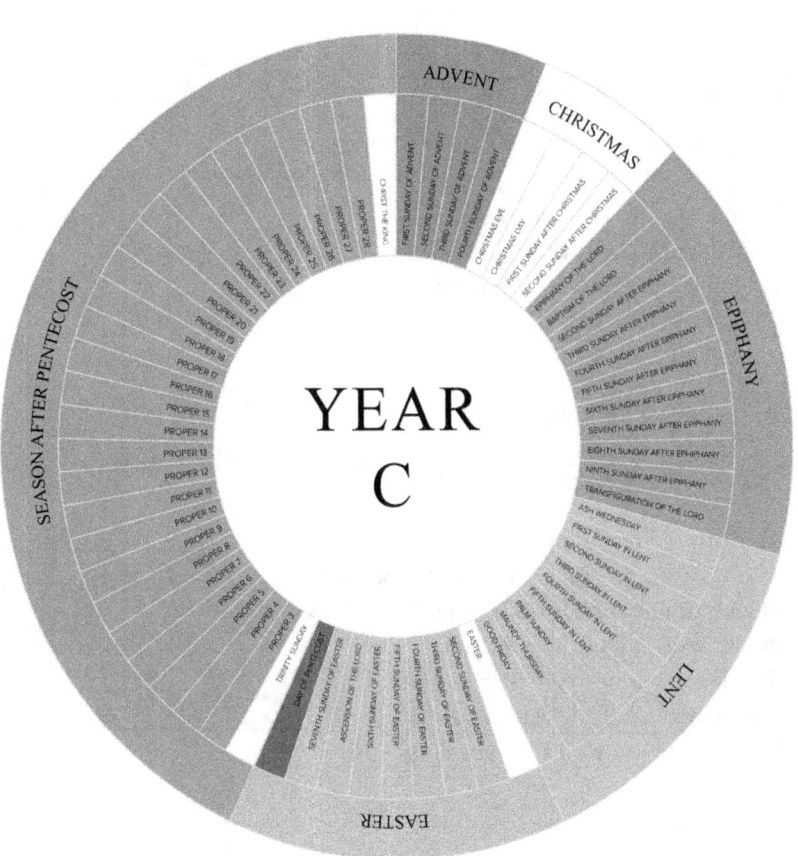

First Sunday of Advent (Year C)

LECTIONARY READINGS

Jeremiah 33:14–16
Psalm 25:1–10
1 Thessalonians 3:9–13
Luke 21:25–36

CALL TO WORSHIP

Psalm 25:1, 5

To you, O Lord, I lift up my soul.
Lead me in your truth, and teach me,
for you are the God of my salvation;
for you I wait all day long.

PRAYER OF RENEWAL

Based on 1 Thessalonians 3:11–13

Lord Jesus, direct our way to you.
May we, your people, increase and abound
in love for one another and for all,
just as we abound in love for you.
Strengthen our hearts in holiness
that we may be blameless before you
when you return with all your saints. Amen.

AFFIRMATION OF FAITH

Based on Luke 21:25, 27–28, 34, 36

What do we believe concerning Jesus' return and how we should live until that time?

We believe that when Jesus returns there will be signs
in the sun, the moon, and the stars, and on the earth.
We believe that we will see the Son of Man coming in a cloud with power and great glory.
We believe that when these things begin to take place, our redemption is drawing near.
We believe that we are to be on guard so that our hearts are not weighed down and that the day does not catch us unexpectedly.
We believe that we are to be alert at all times, praying that we may have the strength
to escape all the things that will take place, and to stand before the Son of Man.

Second Sunday of Advent (Year C)

LECTIONARY READINGS

Malachi 3:1–4
Luke 1:68–79
Philippians 1:3–11
Luke 3:1–6

CALL TO WORSHIP

Luke 3:4–6

Prepare the way of the Lord, make his paths straight.
Every valley shall be filled, and every mountain and hill shall be made low, and the crooked shall be made straight, and the rough ways made smooth; and all flesh shall see the salvation of God.

PRAYER OF RENEWAL

Based on Philippians 1:6, 9–11

Sovereign God,
we know that you, who began a good work among us,
will bring it to completion by the day of Jesus Christ.
May our love overflow more and more with knowledge and full insight
to help us to determine what is best, so that in the day of Christ
we may be pure and blameless, having produced the harvest of righteousness
that comes through Jesus Christ for the glory and praise of God. Amen.

AFFIRMATION OF FAITH

Based on Luke 1:68–79

What do we believe concerning the prophecy of Zechariah?

We believe that the Lord God of Israel looked favorably on his people and redeemed them.
We believe he raised up his Son, Jesus Christ, a mighty savior in the house of David, just as he spoke through the prophets of old.
We believe God saved his people from their enemies, showed them the mercy promised to their ancestors, and remembered his holy covenant, the oath that he swore to our ancestor Abraham.
We believe he raised up John the Baptist, the prophet of the Most High; who went before the Lord to prepare his ways, and to give knowledge of salvation to his people by the forgiveness of their sins.
We believe that by the tender mercy of God, the dawn from on high broke upon his people,
to give light to those who sit in darkness and in the shadow of death, and to guide our feet into the way of peace.

Third Sunday of Advent (Year C)

LECTIONARY READINGS

Zephaniah 3:14–20
Isaiah 12:2–6
Philippians 4:4–7
Luke 3:7–18

CALL TO WORSHIP

Isaiah 12:4–6

Give thanks to the Lord, call on his name;
make known his deeds among the nations; proclaim that his name is exalted.
Sing praises to the Lord, for he has done gloriously;
let this be known in all the earth. Shout aloud and sing for joy, O royal Zion,
for great in your midst is the Holy One of Israel.

PRAYER OF RENEWAL

Based on Zephaniah 3:14–17

Loving God,
during this Advent season,
help us to sing aloud, and rejoice in you with
full and gracious hearts.
We know that you have taken away
the judgments against us,
and that you are in our midst.
When fears overcome us, may we remember
that you delight in us with gladness;
that you quiet us with your love;
that you rejoice over us with singing.
In the name of Jesus we pray. Amen.

AFFIRMATION OF FAITH

Based on Philippians 4:4–7

What do we believe concerning prayer and the peace of God?

We believe we are to rejoice in the Lord always,
and to let our gentleness be known to everyone.
We believe the Lord is near, that we do not worry about anything.
We believe that in everything, we can let our requests
be made known to God through prayer and supplication.
We believe that the peace of God, which surpasses all understanding,
will guard our hearts and our minds in Christ Jesus.

Fourth Sunday of Advent (Year C)

LECTIONARY READINGS

Micah 5:2–5a
Psalm 80:1–7
Hebrews 10:5–10
Luke 1:39–55

CALL TO WORSHIP

Micah 5:2, 4–5a

But you, O Bethlehem of Ephrathah, who are one of the little clans of Judah, from you shall come forth for me one who is to rule in Israel, whose origin is from of old, from ancient days.
And he shall stand and feed his flock in the strength of the Lord, in the majesty of the name of the Lord his God. And they shall live secure, for now he shall be great to the ends of the earth;
and he shall be the one of peace.

PRAYER OF RENEWAL

Based on Luke 1:46–55; Psalm 80:3

Redeeming Lord,
may our souls magnify you alone;
may our spirits rejoice in God our Savior.
Your mercy is for those who fear you
from generation to generation.
You have brought down the powerful
from their thrones, and lifted up the lowly;
you have filled the hungry with good things,
and sent the rich away empty.

Restore us, O God, let your face shine, that we may be saved.
In the name of Jesus we pray. Amen.

AFFIRMATION OF FAITH

Based on Hebrews 10:5–7, 10

What do we believe concerning the sacrifice and obedience of Christ?

We believe that when Christ came into the world, he said,
"Sacrifices and offerings you have not desired, but a body you have prepared for me; in burnt offerings and sin offerings you have taken no pleasure."
We believe he then said, "See, I have come to do your will, O God."
We believe that it is by God's will that we have been sanctified
through the offering of the body of Jesus Christ once for all.

Christmas Eve (Year C)

LECTIONARY READINGS

Isaiah 9:2–7
Psalm 96
Titus 2:11–14
Luke 2:1–20

CALL TO WORSHIP

Psalm 96:7–9

Ascribe to the Lord, O families of the peoples,
ascribe to the Lord glory and strength.
Ascribe to the Lord the glory due his name;
bring an offering, and come into his courts.
Worship the Lord in holy splendor; tremble before him, all the earth.

PRAYER OF RENEWAL

Based on Titus 2:11–14

Lord Jesus,
your grace and your kingdom have appeared,
bringing salvation to all,
and training us to renounce impiety and worldly passions,
and to live lives that are self-controlled, upright, and godly.
We seek to follow you in this way while we wait
for the blessed hope and the manifestation of your glory.
For you gave yourself for us that you might redeem us from all iniquity
and purify for yourself a people who are zealous for good deeds.
In the name of Jesus we pray. Amen.

AFFIRMATION OF FAITH

Based on Isaiah 9:6–7

What do we believe concerning the nature of Jesus' birth and authority?

We believe that a child has been born for us, a son has been given to us.
We believe that authority rests upon his shoulders; and he is named Wonderful Counselor, Mighty God, Everlasting Father, Prince of Peace.
We believe that his authority shall grow continually, and there shall be endless peace for his kingdom. He will establish and uphold it with justice and with righteousness from this time onward and forevermore.

Christmas Day (Year C)

LECTIONARY READINGS

Isaiah 52:7–10
Psalm 98
Hebrews 1:1–12
John 1:1–14

CALL TO WORSHIP

Psalm 98:4–6

Make a joyful noise to the Lord, all the earth;
break forth into joyous song and sing praises.
Sing praises to the Lord with the lyre,
with the lyre and the sound of melody.
With trumpets and the sound of the horn
make a joyful noise before the King, the Lord.

PRAYER OF ADORATION

Based on Isaiah 52:9–10

Holy God,
as we celebrate your birth,
may we come together in song,
for you have comforted and redeemed your people.
You have demonstrated your power
before the eyes of all the nations;
and all the ends of the earth will see the salvation of our God.
We worship and adore you, the Light of the world.
In the name of Jesus we pray. Amen.

AFFIRMATION OF FAITH

Based on John 1:10–13

What do we believe concerning Jesus' coming to this world to bring us salvation?

We believe Jesus was in the world,
and the world came into being through him;
yet the world did not know him.
We believe he came to what was his own,
and his own people did not accept him.
We believe that to all who have received him, who have believed in his name,
he has given the power to become children of God, those born
not of blood or of the will of the flesh or of the will of man, but of God.

First Sunday after Christmas (Year C)

LECTIONARY READINGS

1 Samuel 2:18–20, 26
Psalm 148
Colossians 3:12–17
Luke 2:41–52

CALL TO WORSHIP

Psalm 148:11–14

**Kings of the earth and all peoples, princes and all rulers of the earth!
Young men and women alike, old and young together!**
Let them praise the name of the Lord, for his name alone is exalted;
his glory is above earth and heaven. He has raised up a horn for his people,
praise for all his faithful, for the people of Israel who are close to him. Praise
the Lord!

PRAYER OF RENEWAL

Based on Colossians 3:15–17

Holy God,
let the peace of Christ rule in our hearts,
and help us to be thankful.
Let the word of Christ dwell in us richly;
help us to teach and admonish one another in all wisdom;
and with gratitude in our hearts, may we sing
psalms, hymns, and spiritual songs to you.
And whatever we do, in word or deed,
may we do everything in the name of the Lord Jesus,
giving thanks to you, our Father, through him. Amen.

AFFIRMATION OF FAITH

Based on Colossians 3:12–14

How are we to live as children of God?

We believe that as God's chosen ones, holy and beloved, we are to clothe ourselves with compassion, kindness, humility, meekness, and patience.
We believe we are to bear with one another and, if anyone has a complaint against another,
we are to forgive each other; just as the Lord has forgiven us, so we also must forgive.
We believe that, above all, we are to clothe ourselves with love,
which binds everything together in perfect harmony.

Second Sunday after Christmas (Year C)

LECTIONARY READINGS

Jeremiah 31:7–14
Psalm 147:12–20
Ephesians 1:3–14
John 1:1–18

CALL TO WORSHIP

Ephesians 1:3–4

Blessed be the God and Father of our Lord Jesus Christ,
who has blessed us in Christ
with every spiritual blessing in the heavenly places,
just as he chose us in Christ before the foundation of the world
to be holy and blameless before him in love.

PRAYER OF ADORATION

Based on John 1:1–5, 12, 14

Lord Jesus,
you were in the beginning as the Word, with God, as God.
All things came into being through your mighty power,
and without your presence not one thing came into being.
We praise you for you are life and the light of all people.
Your light shines in the darkness, and the darkness has not overcome it.
In your mercy, you became flesh and lived among us;
and we offer our lives to you, for by your power, we have become children of
God. In the name of Jesus we pray. Amen.

AFFIRMATION OF FAITH

Based on Ephesians 1:5–7, 11–13

What do we believe concerning our adoption, redemption, inheritance, and seal in Christ?

We believe that God predestined us for adoption as his children through Jesus Christ,
according to the good pleasure of his will, to the praise of his glorious grace.
We believe that, in Christ, we have redemption through his blood,
the forgiveness of our trespasses, according to the riches of his grace.
We believe that, in Christ, we have also obtained an inheritance, having been predestined according to the purpose of him who accomplishes all things according to his counsel and will,
so that we, who were the first to set our hope on Christ, might live for the praise of his glory.
We believe that, in Christ, when we heard the word of truth,
the gospel of our salvation, and believed in him,
we were marked with the seal of the promised Holy Spirit.

Epiphany of the Lord (Year C)

LECTIONARY READINGS

Isaiah 60:1–6
Psalm 72:1–7, 10–14
Ephesians 3:1–12
Matthew 2:1–12

CALL TO WORSHIP

Isaiah 60:1–2

Arise, shine; for your light has come,
and the glory of the Lord has risen upon you.
For darkness shall cover the earth, and thick darkness the peoples;
but the Lord will arise upon you, and his glory will appear over you.

PRAYER OF ADORATION

Based on Ephesians 3:1–12

Holy God, we praise you for your word,
allowing us to understand the mystery of Christ:
that we have become fellow heirs,
members of one body, and sharers in the promise
in Christ Jesus through the gospel.
We are so grateful that we have been granted
the good news of the boundless riches of Christ.
We thank you, O Lord, that this was in accordance
with the eternal purpose that you carried out in Christ Jesus our Lord,
in whom we have access to you in boldness
and confidence through faith in Christ.
To him be glory and honor, forever and ever. Amen.

AFFIRMATION OF FAITH

Based on Matthew 2:1–2, 9–11

What do we believe concerning the visit of the wise men?

We believe that, in the time of King Herod, after Jesus was born in Bethlehem of Judea, wise men from the East came to Jerusalem, asking, "Where is the child who has been born king of the Jews? For we observed his star at its rising, and have come to pay him homage."
We believe that they set out for Bethlehem; and there, ahead of them, went the star that they had seen at its rising, until it stopped over the place where the child was. When they saw that the star had stopped, they were overwhelmed with joy.
We believe that on entering the house, they saw the child with Mary his mother; and they knelt down and paid him homage. Then, opening their treasure chests, they offered him gifts of gold, frankincense, and myrrh.

Baptism of the Lord (Year C)

LECTIONARY READINGS

Isaiah 43:1–7
Psalm 29
Acts 8:14–17
Luke 3:15–17, 21–22

CALL TO WORSHIP

Psalm 29:1–2

Ascribe to the Lord, O heavenly beings,
ascribe to the Lord glory and strength.
Ascribe to the Lord the glory of his name;
worship the Lord in holy splendor.

PRAYER OF RENEWAL

Based on Isaiah 43:1–3

Holy God,
we know that we do not need to fear
for you have redeemed us;
you have called us by name, we are yours.
You promise that when we pass
through the waters, you will be with us;
and when we walk through the fire, we shall not be burned,
For you are the Lord our God,
the Holy One of Israel, our Savior. Amen.

AFFIRMATION OF FAITH

Based on Luke 3:15–16, 21–22

What do we believe concerning John the Baptist and Jesus' baptism?

We believe that John the Baptist answered the questions and expectations of the people of his day by saying, "I baptize you with water; but one who is more powerful than I is coming; I am not worthy to untie the thong of his sandals. He will baptize you with the Holy Spirit and fire."

We believe that when Jesus had been baptized and was praying, heaven was opened, and the Holy Spirit descended upon him in bodily form like a dove. And a voice came from heaven, "You are my Son, the Beloved; with you I am well pleased."

Second Sunday after Epiphany (Year C)

LECTIONARY READINGS

Isaiah 62:1–5
Psalm 36:5–10
1 Corinthians 12:1–11
John 2:1–11

CALL TO WORSHIP

Psalm 36:5, 7–9

Your steadfast love, O Lord, extends to the heavens,
your faithfulness to the clouds.
How precious is your steadfast love, O God! All people may take refuge in the shadow of your wings. They feast on the abundance of your house, and you give them drink from the river of your delights. For with you is the fountain of life; in your light we see light.

PRAYER OF RENEWAL

Based on John 2:1–11; Isaiah 62:1–2, 5

Lord Jesus, we believe you are able to perform miracles
in our lives today, just as you turned water to wine long ago.
Do your work of transformation, by the Spirit,
that our lives may reflect your power and your glory;
that the nations may behold the salvation of our God.
May we cling to you each day,
knowing that you pursue us with your steadfast love.
As a bridegroom rejoices over his bride, so you rejoice over your people.
May we live in light of this strong promise. In the name of Jesus, we pray.
Amen.

AFFIRMATION OF FAITH

Based on 1 Corinthians 12:4–11

What do we believe concerning the gifts of the Spirit?

We believe there are varieties of gifts, but the same Spirit; varieties of services, but the same Lord; and varieties of activities, but the same God who activates all of them in everyone.
We believe that to each is given the manifestation of the Spirit for the common good.
We believe that to one is given through the Spirit the utterance of wisdom, and to another the utterance of knowledge according to the same Spirit, to another faith by the same Spirit, to another gifts of healing by the one Spirit, to another the working of miracles, to another prophecy, to another the discernment of spirits, to another various kinds of tongues, to another the interpretation of tongues.
We believe that all these are activated by one and the same Spirit,
who allots to each one individually just as the Spirit chooses.

Third Sunday after Epiphany (Year C)

LECTIONARY READINGS

Nehemiah 8:1–3, 5–6, 8–10
Psalm 19
1 Corinthians 12:12–31a
Luke 4:14–21

CALL TO WORSHIP

Psalm 19:1–4

The heavens are telling the glory of God;
and the firmament proclaims his handiwork.
Day to day pours forth speech, and night to night declares knowledge.
There is no speech, nor are there words; their voice is not heard;
yet their voice goes out through all the earth, and their words to the end
of the world.

PRAYER OF RENEWAL

Based on Psalm 19:7–14

Holy God, we know your law is perfect, reviving the soul;
your decrees are sure, making wise the simple;
your precepts are right, rejoicing the heart;
your commandments are clear, enlightening the eyes;
We know that reverence for you is pure, enduring forever;
your ordinances are true and righteous altogether.
May we desire these things more than gold,
and may our experience of them be sweeter than honey.
Your law protects us; in keeping them there is great reward;
But we confess that we cannot detect all of our errors;
so we ask you to clear us from our hidden faults.

Let the words of our mouths and the meditations of our hearts
be acceptable to you, O Lord, our rock and our redeemer. Amen.

AFFIRMATION OF FAITH

Based on 1 Corinthians 12:12–13, 28

What do we believe concerning the body of Christ?

We believe that just as the body is one and has many members,
and all the members of the body, though many, are one body, so it is with Christ.
We believe that in the one Spirit we were all baptized into one body,
and of the one Spirit, we were all made to drink.
We believe that God has appointed in the church first apostles, second prophets, third teachers; then deeds of power, then gifts of healing, forms of assistance, forms of leadership, and various kinds of tongues.

Fourth Sunday after Epiphany (Year C)

LECTIONARY READINGS

Jeremiah 1:4–10
Psalm 71:1–6
1 Corinthians 13:1–13
Luke 4:21–30

CALL TO WORSHIP

Psalm 71:1–3

In you, O Lord, I take refuge; let me never be put to shame.
In your righteousness deliver me and rescue me;
incline your ear to me and save me.
Be to me a rock of refuge, a strong fortress, to save me,
for you are my rock and my fortress.

PRAYER OF RENEWAL

Based on 1 Corinthians 13:1–7

Gracious Father,
if I speak in the tongues of mortals and of angels,
but do not have love, I am a noisy gong or a clanging cymbal.
And if I have prophetic powers, and understand all mysteries and all knowledge,
and if I have all faith, so as to remove mountains, but do not have love, I am nothing. If I give away all my possessions, and if I hand over my body
so that I may boast, but do not have love, I gain nothing.
Fill me with love that is patient and kind;
with love that is not envious or boastful or arrogant or rude.
Fill me with love that does not insist on its own way; that is not irritable or resentful; that does not rejoice in wrongdoing, but rejoices in the truth.

Fill me with a love that bears all things, believes all things,
hopes all things, endures all things; through Jesus Christ, love incarnate.
Amen.

AFFIRMATION OF FAITH

Based on 1 Corinthians 13:8–12

What do we believe concerning prophecies and knowledge of God?

We believe that love never ends, but as for prophecies, they will come to an end; as for tongues, they will cease; as for knowledge, it will come to an end.
We believe that we know only in part, and we prophesy only in part;
but when the complete comes, the partial will come to an end.
We believe that for now we see in a mirror, dimly, but one day we will see face to face.
Now we know only in part; one day we will know fully, even as we have been fully known.

Fifth Sunday after Epiphany (Year C)

LECTIONARY READINGS

Isaiah 6:1–13
Psalm 138
1 Corinthians 15:1–11
Luke 5:1–11

CALL TO WORSHIP

Isaiah 6:1–3

In the year that King Uzziah died, I saw the Lord sitting on a throne, high and lofty; and the hem of his robe filled the temple. Seraphs were in attendance above him; each had six wings: with two they covered their faces, and with two they covered their feet, and with two they flew.
And one called to another and said:
Holy, holy, holy is the Lord of hosts; the whole earth is full of his glory.

PRAYER OF ADORATION

Based on Psalm 138

Sovereign God,
we give thanks to your name, for your steadfast love and your faithfulness;
for you have exalted your name and your word above everything.
All the kings of the earth shall praise you, O Lord,
for they have heard the words of your mouth.
They shall sing of the ways of the Lord, for great is the glory of the Lord.
Though you are high, you regard the lowly; though we walk in the midst of trouble, you preserve us against the wrath of our enemies;
you stretch out your hand, and your right hand delivers us.
We know you will fulfill your purpose for us; your steadfast love, O Lord, endures forever. We praise you, Father, Son, and Holy Spirit. Amen.

AFFIRMATION OF FAITH

Based on 1 Corinthians 15:3–8

What do we believe concerning the ministry and post-resurrection appearances of Jesus?

We believe that Christ died for our sins, and that he was buried,
and that he was raised on the third day in accordance with the scriptures.
We believe that he appeared to Peter, then to the twelve;
then to more than five hundred brothers and sisters at one time.
Then he appeared to James, and then to all the apostles.
Then, last of all, we believe he appeared to Paul.

Sixth Sunday after Epiphany (Year C)

LECTIONARY READINGS

Jeremiah 17:5–10
Psalm 1
1 Corinthians 15:12–20
Luke 6:17–26

CALL TO WORSHIP

Psalm 1:1–3

Happy are those who do not follow the advice of the wicked,
or take the path that sinners tread, or sit in the seat of scoffers;
but their delight is in the law of the Lord,
and on his law they meditate day and night.
They are like trees planted by streams of water,
which yield their fruit in its season,
and their leaves do not wither. In all that they do, they prosper.

PRAYER OF RENEWAL

Based on Jeremiah 17:5–8

Gracious Lord, we confess that we often rely on
our own strength and resources, and turn away from you.
In doing so our souls remain parched and unsatisfied.
We long to be a people who trust in the Lord, whose trust is the Lord.
We desire to be like trees planted by water, that do not fear when heat comes,
and whose leaves shall stay green; in the year of drought they are not anxious,
and they do not cease to bear fruit.
Help us to be this kind of people; through Jesus Christ our Lord. Amen.

AFFIRMATION OF FAITH

Based on Luke 6:17, 20–23

What did Jesus teach in the sermon on the plain before a great crowd of his disciples and a great multitude of people?

He taught:
Blessed are you who are poor, for yours is the kingdom of God.
Blessed are you who are hungry now, for you will be filled.
Blessed are you who weep now, for you will laugh.
Blessed are you when people hate you, and when they exclude you,
revile you, and defame you on account of the Son of Man.
Rejoice in that day and leap for joy, for surely your reward is great in heaven;
for that is what their ancestors did to the prophets.

Seventh Sunday after Epiphany (Year C)

LECTIONARY READINGS

Genesis 45:3–11, 15
Psalm 37:1–11, 39–40
1 Corinthians 15:35–38, 42–50
Luke 6:27–38

CALL TO WORSHIP

Psalm 37:3–4

Trust in the Lord, and do good;
so you will live in the land, and enjoy security.
Take delight in the Lord,
and he will give you the desires of your heart.

PRAYER OF RENEWAL

Based on Psalm 37:3–7

Faithful God,
help us to trust in you and do good;
that we might dwell in the safety of your presence.
May we take delight in you,
knowing that we will receive the true desires of our heart.
By your grace, may we commit our way to you;
trust in you, and watch you move in your lives.
We know that you have the power to make things right,
and that the justice of our cause will shine like the noonday sun.
Help us to be still and wait patiently for you;
through Jesus Christ our Lord. Amen.

AFFIRMATION OF FAITH

Based on Luke 6:27–28, 31, 37–38

What do we believe Jesus taught concerning how to treat others?

We believe Jesus taught:
"Love your enemies, do good to those who hate you,
bless those who curse you, pray for those who abuse you."
We believe Jesus taught:
"Do to others as you would have them do to you."
We believe Jesus taught:
"Do not judge, and you will not be judged; do not condemn, and you will not be condemned. Forgive, and you will be forgiven; give, and it will be given to you."

Eighth Sunday after Epiphany (Year C)

LECTIONARY READINGS

Isaiah 55:10–13
Psalm 92:1–4, 12–15
1 Corinthians 15:51–58
Luke 6:39–49

CALL TO WORSHIP

Psalm 92:1–4

It is good to give thanks to the Lord,
to sing praises to your name, O Most High;
to declare your steadfast love in the morning, and your faithfulness by night,
to the music of the lute and the harp, to the melody of the lyre.
For you, O Lord, have made me glad by your work;
at the works of your hands I sing for joy.

PRAYER OF RENEWAL

Based on Isaiah 55:10–11; Luke 6:41, 48

Gracious God,
as the rain and snow come down
from heaven and water the earth,
may your word saturate us and fill us, your people,
that we may bear fruit for your kingdom.
By your grace, help us to see and address the log in our own eye
before we point out the speck in our neighbor's eye.
May we build our faith on a firm foundation
so that when the trials and challenges of life come our way
we will not be shaken, for our hope is built on Christ, the solid rock.
In the name of Jesus we pray. Amen.

AFFIRMATION OF FAITH

Based on 1 Corinthians 15:51–53, 58

What do we believe will happen on the day that Jesus returns?

We believe that we will not all die, but we will all be changed,
in a moment, in the twinkling of an eye, at the last trumpet.
We believe that the trumpet will sound,
and the dead will be raised imperishable, and we will be changed.
For this perishable body must put on imperishability,
and this mortal body must put on immortality.
Therefore, we believe we are to be steadfast, immovable, always excelling
in the work of the Lord, because we know that in the Lord our labor is not
in vain.

Ninth Sunday after Epiphany (Year C)

LECTIONARY READINGS

1 Kings 8:22–23, 41–43
Psalm 96:1–9
Galatians 1:1–12
Luke 7:1–10

CALL TO WORSHIP

Psalm 96:1–3

O sing to the Lord a new song;
sing to the Lord, all the earth.
Sing to the Lord, bless his name;
tell of his salvation from day to day.
Declare his glory among the nations,
his marvelous works among all the peoples.

PRAYER OF RENEWAL

Based on Luke 7:1–10

Lord Jesus,
give us the faith of the centurion,
who, though he never saw you, simply said:
"But only speak the word, and let my servant be healed."
As you commended him for his faith and healed his servant,
let us find favor with you and pray according to your will.
May we draw near to you each day,
so that our hearts are in tune with your Holy Spirit,
and our requests are in accord with your kingdom.
In the name of Jesus we pray. Amen.

AFFIRMATION OF FAITH

Based on Galatians 1:7, 9

What do we believe concerning those who preach a false gospel?

We believe that there are some who seek to confuse
God's people and pervert the gospel of Christ.
We believe that if anyone proclaims to us a gospel contrary
to what we have received in God's word, let that one be accursed.

Transfiguration of the Lord (Year C)

LECTIONARY READINGS

Exodus 34:29–35
Psalm 99
2 Corinthians 3:12–4:2
Luke 9:28–43a

CALL TO WORSHIP

Psalm 99:1–3

The Lord is king; let the peoples tremble!
He sits enthroned upon the cherubim; let the earth quake!
The Lord is great in Zion; he is exalted over all the peoples.
Let them praise your great and awesome name. Holy is he!

PRAYER OF RENEWAL

Based on 2 Corinthians 3:17–18; Luke 9:28–29

Lord God,
you revealed your glory to Moses at Mount Sinai;
and to Peter, James, and John on the Mount of Transfiguration.
As your people, we want to know you and behold your glory.
We know that you are Spirit and where
the Spirit of the Lord is, there is freedom.
As we gaze upon you through word, worship, and prayer,
transform us into your image
from one degree of glory to another;
through the power of the Holy Spirit. Amen.

AFFIRMATION OF FAITH

Based on Luke 9:28–36

What do we believe concerning the transfiguration of the Lord?

We believe that one day Jesus took with him Peter and John and James, and went up on a mountain to pray. And while he was praying, the appearance of his face changed, and his clothes became dazzling white.
We believe the disciples saw two men, Moses and Elijah, talking to him. They appeared in glory and were speaking of his departure, which he was about to accomplish at Jerusalem.
We believe a voice from a cloud came and said,
"This is my Son, my Chosen; listen to him!"
We believe that when the voice had spoken, Jesus was found alone;
and the disciples kept silent and told no one any of the things they had seen.

Ash Wednesday (Year C)

LECTIONARY READINGS

Joel 2:1–2, 12–17
Psalm 51:1–17
2 Corinthians 5:20b–6:10
Matthew 6:1–6, 16–21

CALL TO WORSHIP

Joel 2:12–13

Yet even now, says the Lord,
return to me with all your heart,
with fasting, with weeping, and with mourning;
rend your hearts and not your clothing.
Return to the Lord, your God,
for he is gracious and merciful,
slow to anger, and abounding in steadfast love,
and relents from punishing.

PRAYER OF RENEWAL

Based on Psalm 51:15–17; 2 Corinthians 6:6–7

O Lord, open my lips,
and my mouth will declare your praise.
For you have no delight in empty practices.
If I offer a song in vain, you will not be pleased.
The most acceptable gift I have is a broken spirit;
a broken and contrite heart, O God, you will not despise.
During this Lenten season, may we be known by
more than just Sunday morning attendance;

may we be known by purity, knowledge, patience, kindness,
holiness of spirit, genuine love, truthful speech, and the power of God.
In the name of Jesus we pray. Amen.

AFFIRMATION OF FAITH

Based on Matthew 6:3–4, 19–21

What do we believe concerning giving alms and storing up treasures?

We believe that when we give alms, we should not let our left hand know what our right hand is doing, so that our alms may be done in secret; and our Father who sees in secret will reward us.
We believe that we should not store up for ourselves treasures on earth, where moth and rust consume and where thieves break in and steal; but store up for ourselves treasures in heaven, where neither moth nor rust consumes and where thieves do not break in and steal. For where our treasure is, there our heart will be also.

First Sunday in Lent (Year C)

LECTIONARY READINGS

Deuteronomy 26:1–11
Psalm 91:1–2, 9–16
Romans 10:8b–13
Luke 4:1–13

CALL TO WORSHIP

Based on Deuteronomy 26:8–9

The Lord brought his people out of Egypt
with a mighty hand and an outstretched arm,
with a display of power, and with signs and wonders.
He brought them into the promised land,
a land flowing with milk and honey.

PRAYER OF RENEWAL

Based on Psalm 91:1–2, 14–16

Holy God,
as your people we are grateful
that we live in the shelter of the Most High,
that we abide in the shadow of the Almighty.
Grant us grace to declare that you are our refuge
and our fortress; our God, in whom we trust.
We rest in knowing you will deliver us;
you will protect those who know your name.
When we call to you, you answer us.
You rescue us and satisfy us with long life; you show us your salvation.
Through Christ, by the power of the Holy Spirit, we pray. Amen.

AFFIRMATION OF FAITH

Based on Romans 10:9–13

What do we believe regarding salvation?

We believe that if you confess with your lips that Jesus is Lord
and believe in your heart that God raised him from the dead,
you will be saved.
We believe there is no distinction between Jew and Greek;
the same Lord is Lord of all and is generous to all who call on him.
For "Everyone who calls on the name of the Lord shall be saved."

Second Sunday in Lent (Year C)

LECTIONARY READINGS

Genesis 15:1–12, 17–18
Psalm 27
Philippians 3:17–4:1
Luke 13:31–35

CALL TO WORSHIP

Psalm 27:4, 6

One thing I asked of the Lord, that will I seek after: to live in the house of the Lord all the days of my life, to behold the beauty of the Lord, and to inquire in his temple.
Now my head is lifted up above my enemies all around me, and I will offer in his tent sacrifices with shouts of joy; I will sing and make melody to the Lord.

PRAYER OF RENEWAL

Based on Genesis 15:1–12, 17–18; Psalm 27:1, 14

Faithful God,
we know we can trust in you and your word to us.
In spite of his bleak circumstances,
you promised Abraham that his descendants
would be as numerous as the stars in the heavens,
and that promise was fulfilled.
Fill us with faith to look beyond the impossible,
and to trust in your mighty provision and care.
You are our light and our salvation; whom shall we fear?
You are the stronghold of our lives; of whom shall we be afraid?

Fill us with strength and courage as we wait on you.
In the name of Jesus we pray. Amen.

AFFIRMATION OF FAITH

Based on Philippians 3:20–21

What do we believe regarding our true citizenship, the return of Christ, and the redemption of our bodies?

We believe our citizenship is in heaven,
and it is from there that we are expecting a Savior, the Lord Jesus Christ.
We believe he will transform the body of our humiliation
that it may be conformed to the body of his glory.

Third Sunday in Lent (Year C)

LECTIONARY READINGS

Isaiah 55:1–9
Psalm 63:1–8
1 Corinthians 10:1–13
Luke 13:1–9

CALL TO WORSHIP

Based Isaiah 55:1–2

Come, everyone who thirsts, come to the waters;
and you that have no money, come, buy and eat!
Come, buy wine and milk without money and without price.
Why do you spend your money for that which is not bread,
and your labor for that which does not satisfy?
Come and eat what is good, and delight yourselves in rich food.

PRAYER OF RENEWAL

Based on Psalm 63:1–8

O God, you are our God, we long to seek you.
May our souls thirst for you; and our flesh faint for you,
as in a dry and weary land where there is no water.
As we enter our times of worship,
may we gaze upon you and behold your power and glory.
Because your steadfast love is better than life, our lips will praise you.
Throughout our day and week,
stir us to lift up our hands and call on your name.
May our souls be satisfied as with a rich feast,
and may our mouths praise you with joyful lips
when we think of you throughout the day and night;

for you have been our help, and in the shadow of your wings we sing for joy.
Our souls cling to you; your right hand upholds us.
In the name of Jesus we pray. Amen.

AFFIRMATION OF FAITH

Based on 1 Corinthians 10:13

What do we believe about God in the midst of testing and temptation?

We believe God is faithful, and he will not let us be tested beyond our strength, but with the testing he will also provide the way out so that we may be able to endure it.

Fourth Sunday in Lent (Year C)

LECTIONARY READINGS

Joshua 5:9–12
Psalm 32
2 Corinthians 5:16–21
Luke 15:1–3, 11b–32

CALL TO WORSHIP

Psalm 32:11

Be glad in the Lord and rejoice, O righteous.
Shout for joy, all you upright in heart.

PRAYER OF RENEWAL

Based on Psalm 32:7–9; Luke 15:11–32

Merciful God,
we confess that our hearts are often full of deceit.
You offer us counsel and instruction,
but we do not listen to your word.
You offer us wisdom and peace,
but our stubbornness, pride, and short tempers
keep us from true understanding.
Like the prodigal son, we can run after things that do not satisfy;
forgive our wayward hearts.
Like the elder brother, we can be self-righteous and ungrateful;
forgive our hard hearts.
Restore us, O God; be our hiding place;
preserve us from trouble; surround us with glad cries of deliverance.
In the name of Christ, we pray. Amen.

AFFIRMATION OF FAITH

Based on 2 Corinthians 5:17–21

What do we believe concerning our new position in Christ?

We believe that if anyone is in Christ, that person is a new creation:
everything old has passed away; everything has become new.
We believe that God has reconciled us to himself through Christ,
and has given us the ministry of reconciliation.
We believe we are ambassadors for Christ, since God is making his appeal through us.
For our sake, we believe that God made him to be sin who knew no sin,
so that in him we might become the righteousness of God.

Fifth Sunday in Lent (Year C)

LECTIONARY READINGS

Isaiah 43:16–21
Psalm 126
Philippians 3:4b–14
John 12:1–8

CALL TO WORSHIP

Isaiah 43:20–21

I will make a way in the wilderness and rivers in the desert,
to give drink to my chosen people,
the people whom I formed for myself so that they might declare my praise.

PRAYER OF RENEWAL

Based on Psalm 126:4–6; John 12:1–8

Restore us, O Lord,
like streams in the desert.
May those who plant in tears
reap with shouts of joy.
Like Mary, may we be extravagant
in our love and worship of you.
Give us generous hearts
that long to serve our neighbors
and reach out to those who do not know you.
In your holy name we pray. Amen.

AFFIRMATION OF FAITH

Based on Philippians 3:7–9

What do we believe concerning the value of knowing Christ?

We believe that whatever gains we had,
these we have come to regard as loss because of Christ.
We believe we are to regard everything as loss
because of the surpassing value of knowing Christ Jesus our Lord,
being found in him, not having a righteousness of our own that comes from
the law, but one that comes through faith in Christ,
the righteousness from God based on faith.

Palm Sunday (Year C)

LECTIONARY READINGS

Isaiah 50:4–9a
Psalm 118:1–2, 19–29
Philippians 2:5–11
Luke 19:28–40

CALL TO WORSHIP

Luke 19:38

Blessed is the king who comes in the name of the Lord!
Peace in heaven and glory in the highest!

PRAYER OF THANKSGIVING

Based on Psalm 118:1–2, 21–24, 26, 29

O Lord, we give you thanks for you are good;
your steadfast love endures forever!
We thank you that you answer us
and have become our salvation.
We know that Jesus, who was rejected,
has become the chief cornerstone.
This is your doing, O Lord, and it is marvelous in our eyes.
As your people, may we proclaim:
This is the day that the Lord has made;
let us rejoice and be glad in it.
And give us hearts that declare:
Blessed is the one who comes in the name of the Lord.
We give you thanks, for you are good, your steadfast love endures forever.
In the name of the Father, Son, and Holy Spirit. Amen.

AFFIRMATION OF FAITH

Based on Philippians 2:5–11

What do we believe concerning the humility and exaltation of Christ Jesus?

We believe that Jesus, who, though he was in the form of God,
did not regard equality with God as something to be exploited,
but emptied himself, taking the form of a slave, being born in human likeness.
We believe that, being found in human form, he humbled himself
and became obedient to the point of death—even death on a cross.
We believe, therefore, that God also highly exalted him
and gave him the name that is above every name, so that at the name of Jesus
every knee should bend, in heaven and on earth and under the earth,
and every tongue should confess that Jesus Christ is Lord, to the glory of
God the Father.

Maundy Thursday (Year C)

LECTIONARY READINGS

Exodus 12:1–14
Psalm 116:1–2, 12–19
1 Corinthians 11:23–26
John 13:1–17, 31b–35

CALL TO WORSHIP

Psalm 116:12–14

What shall I return to the Lord for all his bounty to me?
I will lift up the cup of salvation and call on the name of the Lord,
I will pay my vows to the Lord in the presence of all his people.

PRAYER OF RENEWAL

Based on John 13:3–5, 14–16

Lord Jesus,
help us to take up the basin and towel,
following your example of servanthood.
May we not seek to make a name for ourselves,
but look for ways to honor and esteem others,
and minister to those around us.
In humility, let your grace so fill our lives that we find joy
in showing compassion to those who are hurting,
in giving of our time to those in need,
in advocating for those who have been treated unjustly.
In the name of Jesus we pray. Amen.

AFFIRMATION OF FAITH

Based on 1 Corinthians 11:23–26

What do we believe concerning the institution of the Lord's Supper?

We believe that the Lord Jesus on the night when he was betrayed
took a loaf of bread, and, when he had given thanks, he broke it and said,
"This is my body that is for you. Do this in remembrance of me."
We believe that in the same way he took the cup also,
after supper, saying, "This cup is the new covenant in my blood.
Do this, as often as you drink it, in remembrance of me."
We believe that as often as we eat the bread and drink the cup,
we proclaim the Lord's death until he comes.

Good Friday (Year B)

LECTIONARY READINGS

Isaiah 52:13–53:12
Psalm 22
Hebrews 4:14–16; 5:7–9
John 18:1–19:42

CALL TO WORSHIP

Hebrews 4:14–16

Since, then, we have a great high priest who has passed through the heavens, Jesus, the Son of God, let us hold fast to our confession. For we do not have a high priest who is unable to sympathize with our weaknesses, but we have one who in every respect has been tested as we are, yet without sin. Let us therefore approach the throne of grace with boldness, so that we may receive mercy and find grace to help in time of need.

PRAYER OF ADORATION

Based on Psalm 22:22–24; Hebrews 5:7–9

Lord Jesus,
you are our Prophet, who tells of your
Father's name to your brothers and sisters
You are our High Priest, our true Worship Leader,
who mediates and inhabits the praise of your people.
We stand in awe of you.
Though you were in anguish in the garden,
the Father heard you when you cried to him.
Though you suffered and died on the cross,
you have become the source of eternal salvation for all who obey you.
In the name of Jesus we pray. Amen.

AFFIRMATION OF FAITH

Based on John 19:38–42

What do we believe concerning the burial of Jesus?

We believe that Joseph of Arimathea, who was a disciple of Jesus, though a secret one because of his fear of the Jews, asked Pilate to let him take away the body of Jesus. Pilate gave him permission; so he came and removed his body.
We believe that Nicodemus, who had at first come to Jesus by night, also came, bringing a mixture of myrrh and aloes, weighing about a hundred pounds.
We believe the two men took the body of Jesus and wrapped it with the spices in linen cloths, according to the burial custom of the Jews. There was a garden in the place where he was crucified, and in the garden there was a new tomb in which no one had ever been laid. And so, because it was the Jewish day of Preparation, and the tomb was nearby, they laid Jesus there.

Easter (Year C)

LECTIONARY READINGS

Isaiah 65:17–25
Psalm 118:1–2, 14–24
1 Corinthians 15:19–26
Luke 24:1–12

CALL TO WORSHIP

Isaiah 65:17–18

I am about to create new heavens and a new earth;
the former things shall not be remembered or come to mind.
But be glad and rejoice forever in what I am creating;
for I am about to create Jerusalem as a joy, and its people as a delight.

PRAYER OF RENEWAL

Based on Luke 24:1–9; Psalm 118:14

Risen Lord,
we know that you are making all things new,
but too often, like the women who first came to the empty tomb,
we are perplexed and confused by your ways.
We doubt your goodness and the promises in your word.
Fill us with faith to believe all that you have revealed
to us about your grace and your steadfast love.
May we sing boldly with the psalmist:
The Lord is our strength and our might;
he has become our salvation;
through Jesus Christ, our living Savior. Amen.

AFFIRMATION OF FAITH

1 Corinthians 15:20–22

What do we believe concerning the resurrection?

We believe that Christ was raised from the dead,
the first fruits of those who have died.
We believe that since death came through a human being,
the resurrection of the dead has also come through a human being;
for as all die in Adam, so all will be made alive in Christ.

Second Sunday of Easter (Year C)

LECTIONARY READINGS

Acts 5:27–32
Psalm 150
Revelation 1:4–8
John 20:19–31

CALL TO WORSHIP

Psalm 150

Praise the Lord! Praise God in his sanctuary;
praise him in his mighty firmament!
Praise him for his mighty deeds;
praise him according to his surpassing greatness!
Praise him with trumpet sound; praise him with lute and harp!
Praise him with tambourine and dance; praise him with strings and pipe!
Praise him with clanging cymbals; praise him with loud clashing cymbals!
Let everything that has breath praise the Lord!

PRAYER OF RENEWAL

Based on John 20:19–31

Lord Jesus,
we are grateful that you are present among your people;
that you have given us the Holy Spirit
to be our Advocate and Teacher.
Help us to forgive others as we have been forgiven.
As with Thomas, remove our doubts and fears and grant us peace.
Give us faith to believe in what we do not see;
that we may have life in your name. Amen.

AFFIRMATION OF FAITH

Based on Revelation 1:5–8

What do we believe concerning the church and the return of Christ?

We believe that Jesus loves us and has freed us from our sins by his blood,
and has made us to be a kingdom, priests serving his God and Father.
We believe all glory and dominion belong to him forever and ever.
We believe that one day he will be coming with the clouds;
and every eye will see him, even those who pierced him;
and on his account all the tribes of the earth will wail.
We believe Jesus is the Alpha and the Omega,
the one who is and who was and who is to come.

Third Sunday of Easter (Year C)

LECTIONARY READINGS

Acts 9:1–20
Psalm 30
Revelation 5:11–14
John 21:1–19

CALL TO WORSHIP

Psalm 30:4–5

Sing praises to the Lord, O you his faithful ones,
and give thanks to his holy name.
For his anger is but for a moment; his favor is for a lifetime.
Weeping may linger for the night, but joy comes with the morning.

PRAYER OF RENEWAL

Based on Acts 9:1–20; John 21:15–17

Holy God, we confess that, like Paul,
we often go about our lives with misdirected zeal.
Thinking we are ministering in your name,
we harbor murder and hatred in our hearts.
Forgive us, O God, and cleanse us of all unrighteousness.
Show us your glory and, by your grace,
remove our spiritual blindness that we would see
all the ways we fail to love you and others.
Like Peter, restore us and make us whole.
Help us to feed your sheep, care for the hurting,
and reach out to the lost with good news of new life. Amen.

AFFIRMATION OF FAITH

Based on Revelation 5:11–13

What do we believe concerning John's vision of heaven?

We believe he heard the voice of many angels surrounding the throne
and the living creatures and the elders.
We believe they numbered myriads of myriads
and thousands of thousands, and were singing with full voice,
"Worthy is the Lamb that was slaughtered to receive power
and wealth and wisdom and might and honor and glory and blessing!"
We believe he heard every creature in heaven and on earth
and under the earth and in the sea, and all that is in them, singing,
"To the one seated on the throne and to the Lamb
be blessing and honor and glory and might forever and ever!"

Fourth Sunday of Easter (Good Shepherd Sunday, Year C)

LECTIONARY READINGS

Acts 9:36–43
Psalm 23
Revelation 7:9–17
John 10:22–30

CALL TO WORSHIP

Revelation 7:9–12

After this I looked, and there was a great multitude that no one could count, from every nation, from all tribes and peoples and languages, standing before the throne and before the Lamb, robed in white, with palm branches in their hands. They cried out in a loud voice, saying,
"Salvation belongs to our God who is seated on the throne, and to the Lamb!"
And all the angels stood around the throne and around the elders and the four living creatures,
and they fell on their faces before the throne and worshiped God, singing,
"Amen! Blessing and glory and wisdom and thanksgiving and honor and power and might be to our God forever and ever! Amen."

PRAYER OF RENEWAL

Based on Psalm 23

Jesus, you are my Good Shepherd, I shall not want.
You let me rest in green pastures;
you lead me beside still waters; you restore my soul.
You lead me in right paths for your name's sake.

Even though I walk through the darkest valley,
I fear no evil; for you are with me;
your rod and your staff—they comfort me.
You prepare a table before me in the presence of my enemies;
you anoint me head with oil; my cup overflows.
Surely goodness and mercy shall follow me all the days of my life,
and I shall dwell in the house of the Lord forever. Amen.

AFFIRMATION OF FAITH

Based on John 10:27–28

What do we believe concerning Jesus, our Good Shepherd?

We believe Jesus' sheep, his people, hear his voice. He knows them, and they follow him.
We believe he will give them eternal life, and they will never perish.
We believe that no one will snatch them out of his hand.

Fifth Sunday of Easter (Year C)

LECTIONARY READINGS

Acts 11:1–18
Psalm 148
Revelation 21:1–6
John 13:31–35

CALL TO WORSHIP

Based Psalm 148:1–4

Praise the Lord! Praise the Lord from the heavens; praise him in the heights!
Praise him, all his angels; praise him, all his host!
Praise him, sun and moon; praise him, all you shining stars!
Praise him, you highest heavens, and you waters above the heavens!

PRAYER OF RENEWAL

Based on Acts 11:1–18; John 13:34–35

Gracious God,
we know you bring life and salvation
to all who call on your name.
We thank you that you do not count anyone greater than another,
for the ground is level at the foot of the cross.
We are all in need of your cleansing blood and forgiving grace.
Help us to live in light of your redemption.
and to love one another just as you have loved us.
May the world know that we are your disciples
by the love we have for one another.
In the name of Jesus we pray. Amen.

AFFIRMATION OF FAITH

Based on Revelation 21:1–6

What do we believe concerning John's vision of a new heaven and a new earth?

We believe he saw the holy city, the new Jerusalem,
coming down out of heaven from God, prepared as a bride adorned for her husband.
We believe he heard a loud voice from the throne saying,
"See, the home of God is among mortals. He will dwell with them; they will be his peoples, and God himself will be with them; he will wipe every tear from their eyes. Death will be no more; mourning and crying and pain will be no more, for the first things have passed away."
We believe he heard the one who was seated on the throne say,
"See, I am making all things new. It is done! I am the Alpha and the Omega, the beginning and the end. To the thirsty I will give water as a gift from the spring of the water of life."

Sixth Sunday of Easter (Year C)

LECTIONARY READINGS

Acts 16:9–15
Psalm 67
Revelation 21:10, 21:22–22:5
John 14:23–29

CALL TO WORSHIP

Psalm 67:4–5

Let the nations be glad and sing for joy,
for you judge the peoples with equity and guide the nations upon earth.
Let the peoples praise you, O God; let all the peoples praise you.

PRAYER OF RENEWAL

Based on John 14:23–29; Psalm 67:7

Sovereign Lord,
help us to keep your word.
May our Advocate, the Holy Spirit,
teach us in all things and remind us
of your presence and power, and may he give us peace.
Let not our hearts be troubled, nor let us be be afraid,
for we know that you are seated with the Father in heaven,
and that you are with us and for us and will never leave us.
May you continue to bless us, O Lord,
and may all the ends of the earth praise your name. Amen.

AFFIRMATION OF FAITH

Based on Revelation 21:10, 22–27

What do we believe concerning John's vision of the holy city?

We believe the spirit carried John away to a great, high mountain and showed him the holy city Jerusalem coming down out of heaven from God. We believe he saw no temple in the city, for its temple is the Lord God the Almighty and the Lamb. And the city has no need of sun or moon to shine on it, for the glory of God is its light, and its lamp is the Lamb.
We believe the nations will walk by its light, and the kings of the earth will bring their glory into it.
Its gates will never be shut by day—and there will be no night there.
We believe people will bring into the city the glory and the honor of the nations. Nothing unclean will enter it, nor anyone who practices abomination or falsehood, but only those who are written in the Lamb's book of life.

Ascension of the Lord (Year C)

LECTIONARY READINGS

Acts 1:1-11
Psalm 47
Ephesians 1:15-23
Luke 24:44-53

CALL TO WORSHIP

Psalm 47:5-6

God has gone up with a shout, the Lord with the sound of a trumpet.
Sing praises to God, sing praises; sing praises to our King, sing praises.

PRAYER OF RENEWAL

Based on Ephesians 1:17-21

Father of glory, we confess that we often
disregard your power at work in our lives.
Give us a spirit of wisdom and revelation as we come to know Christ.
We confess that we often forget your promises.
Enlighten the eyes of our heart that we may know the hope to which you
have called us, the riches of Christ's glorious inheritance among his people,
and the immeasurable greatness of Christ's power for us who believe.
We thank you that you put this power to work in Christ
when you raised him from the dead and seated him
at your right hand in the heavenly places.
Help us to live in light of Christ's greatness every day—
to acknowledge that he is far above all rule and authority and power and
dominion,
and that his name is above every name, not only in this age, but also in the
age to come. For the glory of your ascended Son. Amen.

AFFIRMATION OF FAITH

Based on Acts 1:3, 8, 11

What do we believe concerning the earthly appearances and the heavenly ascension of our Lord?

We believe that after he suffered, Jesus presented himself alive to the apostles by many convincing proofs, appearing to them during forty days and speaking about the kingdom of God.
We believe that, like the apostles, we receive power through the Holy Spirit, and that we, the church, are called to be Christ's witnesses to the ends of the earth.
We believe that Jesus, who was taken up to heaven,
will come again in the same way he departed.

Seventh Sunday of Easter (Year C)

LECTIONARY READINGS

Acts 16:16–34
Psalm 97
Revelation 22:12–14, 16–17, 20–21
John 17:20–26

CALL TO WORSHIP

Psalm 97:1, 11–12

The Lord is king! Let the earth rejoice;
let the many coastlands be glad!
Light dawns for the righteous,
and joy for the upright in heart.
Rejoice in the Lord, O you righteous,
and give thanks to his holy name!

PRAYER OF RENEWAL

Based on John 17:20–24; Revelation 22:16–17

Lord Jesus, our High Priest,
you prayed that your followers may all be one,
so that the world may know the love you have for us.
You also prayed that we may be with you and see your glory.
Lead us to your glorious throne in heaven,
and help us to seek the things which are above.
We want to draw closer and closer to you, O Lord,
for you are the root and the descendant of David, the bright morning star,
You call everyone who is thirsty to come.

Therefore, let us drink from your living water
and be filled with the gift of your Holy Spirit.
In the name of Jesus we pray. Amen.

AFFIRMATION OF FAITH

Based on Revelation 22:12–13

What do we believe concerning Jesus' preeminence and return?

We believe Jesus said, "I am coming soon; my reward is with me,
to repay according to everyone's work."
We believe Jesus said, "I am the Alpha and the Omega,
the first and the last, the beginning and the end."

Day of Pentecost (Year C)

LECTIONARY READINGS

Acts 2:1–21
Psalm 104:24–35
Romans 8:14–17
John 14:8–17, 25–27

CALL TO WORSHIP

Psalm 104:31–33

May the glory of the Lord endure forever; may the Lord rejoice in his works—
who looks on the earth and it trembles,
who touches the mountains and they smoke.
I will sing to the Lord as long as I live; I will sing praise to my God while I have being.

PRAYER OF RENEWAL

Based on John 14:8–17, 25–27

Lord Jesus,
as children of God,
if we know you, we know the Father.
We are grateful that your word still speaks to us,
leading us and guiding us.
We are thankful that when we ask for anything in your name
you hear us and answer our prayers.
Help us to keep your commandments out of love for you.
Thank you for our Advocate, the promised Holy Spirit,
who leads us into all truth,
and who abides with us forever.
In the name of Jesus we pray. Amen.

AFFIRMATION OF FAITH

Based on Romans 8:14–17

What do we believe concerning our adoption as sons and daughters of God?

We believe that all who are led by the Spirit of God are children of God.
We believe, therefore, that we did not receive a spirit of slavery
to fall back into fear, but we have received a spirit of adoption.
We believe that when we cry "Abba! Father!" it is that very Spirit
bearing witness with our spirit that we are children of God,
and if children, then heirs, heirs of God and joint heirs with Christ—
if, in fact, we suffer with him so that we may also be glorified with him.

Trinity Sunday (Year C)

LECTIONARY READINGS

Proverbs 8:1–4, 22–31
Psalm 8
Romans 5:1–5
John 16:12–15

CALL TO WORSHIP

Psalm 8:1–2, 9

O Lord, our Sovereign, how majestic is your name in all the earth!
You have set your glory above the heavens.
Out of the mouth of babies and infants,
you have established strength because of your foes,
to still the enemy and the avenger.
O Lord, our Sovereign, how majestic is your name in all the earth!

PRAYER OF THANKSGIVING

Based on Romans 5:1–5

Triune God, we are grateful that we are justified by faith,
and that we have peace with with you.
We stand in your grace,
and we boast in our hope of sharing in your glory.
We also boast in our sufferings,
knowing that suffering produces endurance,
and endurance produces character, and character produces hope.
Thank you, Lord, that this hope does not disappoint us,
because your love has been poured into our hearts
through the Holy Spirit that has been given to us.
In the name of the Father, the Son, and the Holy Spirit, we pray. Amen.

AFFIRMATION OF FAITH

Based on John 16:12–15

What do we believe concerning the Holy Spirit?

We believe that the Spirit guides us into all truth.
We believe that he does not speak on his own,
but he speaks whatever he hears and declares to us the things that are to come.
We believe that he glorifies Jesus because the Spirit takes what is Christ's and declares it to us.

Proper 3 (Year C)

Sunday between May 24 and May 28 inclusive

LECTIONARY READINGS

Isaiah 55:10–13
Psalm 92:1–4, 12–15
1 Corinthians 15:51–58
Luke 6:39–49

CALL TO WORSHIP

Psalm 92:1–4

It is good to give thanks to the Lord,
to sing praises to your name, O Most High;
to declare your steadfast love in the morning, and your faithfulness by night,
to the music of the lute and the harp, to the melody of the lyre.
For you, O Lord, have made me glad by your work;
at the works of your hands I sing for joy.

PRAYER OF RENEWAL

Based on Isaiah 55:10–11; Luke 6:41, 48

Gracious God, as the rain and snow
come down from heaven and water the earth,
may your word saturate us and fill us, your people,
that we may bear fruit for your kingdom.
By your grace, help us to see and address the log in our own eye
before we point out the speck in our neighbor's eye.
May we build our faith on a firm foundation
so that when the trials and challenges of life come our way
we will not be shaken, for our hope is built on Christ, the solid rock.
In the name of Jesus we pray. Amen.

AFFIRMATION OF FAITH

Based on 1 Corinthians 15:51–53, 58

What do we believe will happen on the day that Jesus returns?

We believe that we will not all die, but we will all be changed,
in a moment, in the twinkling of an eye, at the last trumpet.
We believe that the trumpet will sound,
and the dead will be raised imperishable, and we will be changed.
For this perishable body must put on imperishability,
and this mortal body must put on immortality.
Therefore, we believe we are to be steadfast, immovable, always excelling
in the work of the Lord, because we know that in the Lord our labor is not
in vain.

Proper 4 (Year C)

Sunday between May 29 and June 4 inclusive

LECTIONARY READINGS

1 Kings 8:22–23, 41–43
Psalm 96:1–9
Galatians 1:1–12
Luke 7:1–10

CALL TO WORSHIP

Psalm 96:1–3

O sing to the Lord a new song;
sing to the Lord, all the earth.
Sing to the Lord, bless his name;
tell of his salvation from day to day.
Declare his glory among the nations,
his marvelous works among all the peoples.

PRAYER OF RENEWAL

Based on Luke 7:1–10

Lord Jesus,
give us the faith of the centurion,
who, though he never saw you, simply said:
"But only speak the word, and let my servant be healed."
As you commended him for his faith and healed his servant,
let us find favor with you and pray according to your will.
May we draw near to you each day,
so that our hearts are in tune with your Holy Spirit,
and our requests are in accord with your kingdom.
In the name of Jesus we pray. Amen.

AFFIRMATION OF FAITH

Based on Galatians 1:7, 9

What do we believe concerning those we preach a false gospel?

We believe that there are some who seek to confuse
God's people and pervert the gospel of Christ.
We believe that if anyone proclaims to us a gospel contrary
to what we have received in God's word, let that one be accursed.

Proper 5 (Year C)

Sunday between June 5 and June 11 inclusive

LECTIONARY READINGS

1 Kings 17:17–24
Psalm 30
Galatians 1:11–24
Luke 7:11–17

CALL TO WORSHIP

Psalm 30:4–5

Sing praises to the Lord, O you his faithful ones,
and give thanks to his holy name.
For his anger is but for a moment; his favor is for a lifetime.
Weeping may linger for the night, but joy comes with the morning.

PRAYER OF RENEWAL

Based on Luke 7:11–17

Lord Jesus,
in your love and compassion,
you heal the sick and raise the dead.
Have mercy on us, O Lord,
and breathe new life into our hearts
when they grow cold and complacent.
We confess that, too often, we turn to created things
rather than the Creator to quench our thirsty souls.
By your grace, may we repent and return to you once again,
the one who calls us from death to life.
In the name of Jesus we pray. Amen.

AFFIRMATION OF FAITH

Based on Galatians 1:18–24

What do we believe concerning Paul's early ministry and his first visit with Peter?

We believe that three years after his conversion, Paul went to Jerusalem to visit Peter and stayed with him fifteen days; but he did not see any other apostle except James the Lord's brother.
We believe he went into the regions of Syria and Cilicia, and he was still unknown by sight to the churches of Judea; they only heard it said, "The one who formerly was persecuting us is now proclaiming the faith he once tried to destroy."
We believe those believers glorified God because of Paul's testimony.

Proper 6 (Year C)

Sunday between June 12 and June 18 inclusive

LECTIONARY READINGS

2 Samuel 11:26–12:10, 13–15
Psalm 32
Galatians 2:15–21
Luke 7:36–8:3

CALL TO WORSHIP

Psalm 32:10–11

Many are the torments of the wicked,
but steadfast love surrounds those who trust in the Lord.
Be glad in the Lord and rejoice, O righteous,
and shout for joy, all you upright in heart.

PRAYER OF RENEWAL

Based on Luke 7:44–50

Lord Jesus,
you told us that those who know
they have been forgiven much, love much;
but those who believe
they only need to be forgiven little, love little.
Give us hearts that realize
how desperate we truly are for you, O Lord.
Help us not to become self-righteous in our faith;
but fill us with gratitude that we,
like the woman who anointed you with oil,
would be extravagant in our worship and adoration of you.
In the name of Jesus we pray. Amen.

AFFIRMATION OF FAITH

Based on Galatians 2:19–20

What do we believe concerning our life in Christ?

We believe we have been crucified with Christ;
and it is no longer we who live, but it is Christ who lives in us.
We believe that the life we now live in the flesh
we live by faith in the Son of God, who loved us and gave himself for us.

Proper 7 (Year C)

Sunday between June 19 and June 25 inclusive

LECTIONARY READINGS

Isaiah 65:1–9
Psalm 22:19–28
Galatians 3:23–29
Luke 8:26–39

CALL TO WORSHIP

Psalm 22:27–28

All the ends of the earth shall remember and turn to the Lord;
and all the families of the nations shall worship before him.
For dominion belongs to the Lord, and he rules over the nations.

PRAYER OF RENEWAL

Based on Isaiah 65:1–2; Psalm 22:19; Luke 8:34–39

Lord Jesus,
we confess that we are often a rebellious people
who follow our own devices and walk in a way that is not good.
O Lord, in our rebellion, draw near to us and come to our aid.
When we are plagued by spiritual oppression, secrecy, and addictions,
we need you to come to us and heal us.
Bring us out of darkness, restore us, and put us in a healthy state of mind.
And may we be faithful to declare all that you have done for us.
In the name of Jesus we pray. Amen.

AFFIRMATION OF FAITH

Based on Galatians 3:26, 28

What do we believe concerning our identity in Christ?

We believe that in Christ Jesus we are all children of God through faith.
We believe there is no longer Jew or Greek, slave or free,
male and female; for all of us are one in Christ Jesus.

Proper 8 (Year C)

Sunday between June 26 and July 2 inclusive

LECTIONARY READINGS

1 Kings 19:15–16, 19–21
Psalm 16
Galatians 5:1, 13–25
Luke 9:51–62

CALL TO WORSHIP

Psalm 16:7–8

I bless the Lord who gives me counsel; in the night also my heart instructs me.
I keep the Lord always before me;
because he is at my right hand, I shall not be moved.

PRAYER OF ADORATION

Based on Psalm 16

Loving God, in you we take refuge.
You are our chosen portion and our cup; you hold our lot.
We bless you, Lord, for you give us counsel.
May we keep you always before us; so that we shall not be moved.
May our hearts be glad, and may our souls rejoice; may our bodies rest secure.
In your mercy show us the path of life.
Lord, in your presence there is fullness of joy; in your right hand are pleasures forevermore. In the name of Jesus we pray. Amen.

AFFIRMATION OF FAITH

Based on Galatians 5:16–25

What do we believe concerning our life in the Spirit?

We believe that we are to live by the Spirit and not gratify the desires of the flesh. For what the flesh desires is opposed to the Spirit, and what the Spirit desires is opposed to the flesh; for these are opposed to each other, to prevent us from doing what we want.
We believe the works of the flesh are fornication, impurity, licentiousness, idolatry, sorcery, enmities, strife, jealousy, anger, quarrels, dissensions, factions, envy, drunkenness, carousing, and things like these.
By contrast, we believe the fruit of the Spirit is love, joy, peace, patience, kindness, generosity, faithfulness, gentleness, and self-control. Those who belong to Christ Jesus have crucified the flesh with its passions and desires. We believe that if we live by the Spirit, we should also be guided by the Spirit.

Proper 9 (Year C)

Sunday between July 3 and July 9 inclusive

LECTIONARY READINGS

Isaiah 66:10–14
Psalm 66:1–9
Galatians 6:1–16
Luke 10:1–11, 16–20

CALL TO WORSHIP

Psalm 66:1–2, 4–5

Make a joyful noise to God, all the earth;
sing the glory of his name; give to him glorious praise.
**All the earth worships you; and sings praises to you;
they sing praises to your name.
Come and see what God has done:
he is awesome in his deeds among mortals.**

PRAYER OF INTERCESSION

Based on Luke 10:1–11, 16–20

Loving God,
you send us out into the world
to carry the good news of the gospel to those around us.
We know that the harvest is plentiful, but the laborers are few.
May we be obedient to your call,
living each day as your messengers of peace.
Give us wisdom and faith, for we know we will encounter
acceptance and salvation as well as resistance and rejection.

Give us strength and authority over the evil one,
and may your kingdom come with power.
In the name of Jesus we pray. Amen.

AFFIRMATION OF FAITH

Based on Galatians 6:1–2, 7–10

What do we believe concerning restoration and bearing one another's burdens?

We believe that if anyone is detected in a transgression,
we who have received the Spirit should restore such a one in a spirit of gentleness.
We believe we are to bear one another's burdens, and in this way we will fulfill the law of Christ.
We believe that we will reap whatever we sow. If we sow to our own flesh, we will reap corruption from the flesh; but if we sow to the Spirit, we will reap eternal life from the Spirit.
We believe we are not to grow weary in doing what is right; whenever we have an opportunity, we should work for the good of all, and especially for those of the family of faith.

Proper 10 (Year C)

Sunday between July 10 and July 16 inclusive

LECTIONARY READINGS

Deuteronomy 30:9–14
Psalm 25:1–10
Colossians 1:1–14
Luke 10:25–37

CALL TO WORSHIP

Psalm 25:8–10

Good and upright is the Lord; therefore he instructs sinners in the way.
He leads the humble in what is right, and teaches the humble his way.
All the paths of the Lord are steadfast love and faithfulness,
for those who keep his covenant and his decrees.

PRAYER OF RENEWAL

Based on Colossians 1:1–14

Faithful God,
strengthen our faith in your Son, Christ Jesus,
and give us love for all the saints,
because of the hope laid up for us in heaven.
We want the gospel to bear fruit among us
as we truly comprehend the grace of God.
Fill us with the knowledge of your will
in all spiritual wisdom and understanding,
so that we may lead lives that are pleasing to you.
Make us strong with all the strength
that comes from your glorious power,
and may we be prepared to endure everything

with patience, while joyfully giving thanks to you,
for you have rescued us from the power of darkness
and transferred us into the kingdom of your beloved Son,
in whom we have redemption, the forgiveness of sins. Amen.

AFFIRMATION OF FAITH

Based on Deuteronomy 30:14; Luke 10:27

What do we believe concerning the word of God and the law of God?

We believe the word is very near to us; it is in our mouth and in our heart for us to observe.
We believe we shall love the Lord our God with all our heart, and with all our soul, and with all our strength, and with all our mind; and our neighbor as ourselves.

Proper 11 (Year C)

Sunday between July 17 and July 23 inclusive

LECTIONARY READINGS

Genesis 18:1–10a
Psalm 15
Colossians 1:15–28
Luke 10:38–42

CALL TO WORSHIP

Based on Luke 10:38–42

O Lord, as we draw near to you in worship, give us undivided hearts.
Remove our worries and distractions, that we may bow before you,
listening to your voice, choosing your ways. Amen.

PRAYER OF RENEWAL

Based on Psalm 15

Merciful God,
help us to be those who walk blamelessly, and do what is right.
We desire to speak the truth from our hearts;
and not slander with our tongues.
By your grace, may we do no evil to our friends,
nor take up a reproach against our neighbors.
May we despise evil in all its various forms,
but honor those who fear the Lord.
Remove our greed; may we not lend money at interest,
nor take a bribe against the innocent.
As we grow in holiness, by your grace, may we find a firm foundation in you.
In the name of Jesus we pray. Amen.

AFFIRMATION OF FAITH

Based on Colossians 1:15–20

What do we believe concerning the authority of Christ?

We believe Christ is the image of the invisible God, the firstborn of all creation; for in him all things in heaven and on earth were created, things visible and invisible, whether thrones or dominions or rulers or powers—all things have been created through him and for him.
We believe he himself is before all things, and in him all things hold together. We believe he is the head of the body, the church; he is the beginning, the firstborn from the dead, so that he might come to have first place in everything.
We believe that in him all the fullness of God was pleased to dwell, and through him God was pleased to reconcile to himself all things, whether on earth or in heaven, by making peace through the blood of his cross.

Proper 12 (Year C)

Sunday between July 24 and July 30 inclusive

LECTIONARY READINGS

Genesis 18:20–32
Psalm 138
Colossians 2:6–19
Luke 11:1–13

CALL TO WORSHIP

Psalm 138:4–5

All the kings of the earth shall praise you, O Lord,
for they have heard the words of your mouth.
They shall sing of the ways of the Lord,
for great is the glory of the Lord.

PRAYER OF ADORATION

Based on Luke 11:2–4, 9–10

Our Father, hallowed be your name.
Your kingdom come. Give us each day our daily bread.
And forgive us our sins, for we ourselves forgive everyone indebted to us.
And do not bring us to the time of trial.
We know that if we ask, it will be given to us;
if we search, we will find; if we knock, the door will be opened for us.
For everyone who asks receives, and everyone who searches finds,
and for everyone who knocks, the door will be opened.
In the name of Jesus we pray. Amen.

AFFIRMATION OF FAITH

Based on Colossians 2:11–14

What do we believe concerning circumcision, baptism, and salvation?

We believe that in Christ we were circumcised with a spiritual circumcision, by putting off the body of the flesh in the circumcision of Christ.
We believe that when we were buried with Christ in baptism, we were also raised with him through faith in the power of God, who raised him from the dead.
We believe that when we were dead in our trespasses and the uncircumcision of our flesh, God made us alive together with him, when he forgave us all our trespasses, erasing the record that stood against us with its legal demands. He set this aside, nailing it to the cross.

Proper 13 (Year C)

Sunday between July 31 and August 6 inclusive

LECTIONARY READINGS

Ecclesiastes 1:2, 12–14; 2:18–23
Psalm 49:1–12
Colossians 3:1–11
Luke 12:13–21

CALL TO WORSHIP

Colossians 3:1–3

If you have been raised with Christ, seek the things that are above,
where Christ is, seated at the right hand of God.
Set your minds on things that are above, not on things that are on earth,
for you have died, and your life is hidden with Christ in God.

PRAYER OF RENEWAL

Based on Luke 12:13–21; Psalm 49:1–12; Ecclesiastes 2:18–23

Gracious God,
help us to be on our guard against all kinds of greed.
Forgive us for putting our trust in wealth and boasting of our riches
for our lives do not consist in the abundance of possessions.
Forgive us for storing up treasures for ourselves, but not being generous
toward you. By your grace help us to see the vanity in selfish labor
for in the end, we will leave our possessions with others.
In the name of Jesus we pray. Amen.

AFFIRMATION OF FAITH

Based on Colossians 3:5–11

What do we believe concerning evil desires?

We believe we are to put to death whatever is earthly: fornication, impurity, passion, evil desire, and greed (which is idolatry). On account of these the wrath of God is coming on those who are disobedient; and these are the ways we also once followed, when we were living that life.

We believe that we must get rid of all such things—anger, wrath, malice, slander, and abusive language from our mouths.

We believe we are not to lie to one another, seeing that we have stripped off the old self with its practices and have clothed ourselves with the new self, which is being renewed in knowledge according to the image of its creator. In that renewal there is no longer Greek and Jew, circumcised and uncircumcised, slave and free; but Christ is all and in all!

Proper 14 (Year C)

Sunday between August 7 and August 13 inclusive

LECTIONARY READINGS

Genesis 15:1–6
Psalm 33:12–22
Hebrews 11:1–3, 8–16
Luke 12:32–40

CALL TO WORSHIP

Psalm 33:20–22

Our soul waits for the Lord; he is our help and shield.
Our heart is glad in him, because we trust in his holy name.
Let your steadfast love, O Lord, be upon us, even as we hope in you.

PRAYER OF RENEWAL

Based on Luke 12:32–40

Gracious Lord,
help us not to be afraid.
Give us grace to be generous
in our giving and in our love for others.
May we live with a readiness for your return,
with hearts set, not on this world, but on you;
for where our treasure is, there our hearts will be also.
In the name of Jesus we pray. Amen.

AFFIRMATION OF FAITH

Based on Hebrews 11:1–3, 13, 16

What do we believe concerning faith and our spiritual ancestors?

We believe that faith is the assurance of things hoped for, the conviction of things not seen.
We believe it was by faith that our ancestors received approval.
We believe it is by faith that we understand that the worlds were prepared by the word of God,
so that what is seen was made from things that are not visible.
We believe our ancestors confessed that they were strangers and foreigners on the earth.
We believe that they desired a better country, that is, a heavenly one.

Proper 15 (Year C)

Sunday between August 14 and August 20 inclusive

LECTIONARY READINGS

Jeremiah 23:23–29
Psalm 82
Hebrews 11:29–12:2
Luke 12:49–56

CALL TO WORSHIP

Psalm 82:8

Rise up, O God, judge the earth;
for all the nations belong to you!

PRAYER OF RENEWAL

Based on Hebrews 12:1–2

Holy God,
since we are surrounded by so great a cloud of witnesses,
let us also lay aside every weight and the sin that clings so closely,
and let us run with perseverance the race that is set before us,
looking to Jesus the pioneer and perfecter of our faith,
who for the sake of the joy that was set before him endured the cross,
disregarding its shame, and has taken his seat at the right hand of the throne
of God. Amen.

AFFIRMATION OF FAITH

Based on Hebrews 11:29–31, 39–40

What do we believe concerning the power of faith?

We believe that, by faith, God's people passed through the Red Sea
as if it were dry land, but when the Egyptians attempted to do so they were drowned.
We believe that, by faith, the walls of Jericho fell after they had been encircled for seven days.
We believe that, by faith, Rahab the prostitute did not perish with those who were disobedient, because she had received the spies in peace.
We believe that all these, though they were commended for their faith,
did not receive what was promised, since God had provided something better so that they would not, apart from us, be made perfect.

Proper 16 (Year C)

Sunday between August 21 and August 27 inclusive

LECTIONARY READINGS

Isaiah 58:9b–14
Psalm 103:1–8
Hebrews 12:18–29
Luke 13:10–17

CALL TO WORSHIP

Psalm 103:1–5

Bless the Lord, O my soul, and all that is within me, bless his holy name.
Bless the Lord, O my soul, and do not forget all his benefits—who forgives all your iniquity, who heals all your diseases, who redeems your life from the Pit, who crowns you with steadfast love and mercy, who satisfies you with good as long as you live so that your youth is renewed like the eagle's.

PRAYER OF RENEWAL

Based on Isaiah 58:9–14

Redeeming Lord, we call on you; we cry to you for help.
Help us not to point fingers, speaking evil of others,
but offer our food to the hungry and satisfy the needs of the afflicted.
May you guide us continually, and satisfy our needs in parched places.
We want to be like a watered garden, like a spring of water whose waters never fail.
Help us to raise up the foundations of many generations and to bring restoration.
Keep us from trampling the Sabbath, from pursuing our own interests on your holy day.

May we call the Sabbath a delight and honor it, not going our own ways
serving our own interests, or pursuing your own affairs.
By doing this, we shall take delight in you.
In the name of Jesus we pray. Amen.

AFFIRMATION OF FAITH

Based on Hebrews 12:22–24, 28

What do we believe concerning the mystery of our participation in the heavenly assembly?

We believe we have come to Mount Zion and to the city of the living God, the heavenly Jerusalem, and to innumerable angels in festal gathering, and to the assembly of the firstborn who are enrolled in heaven, and to God the judge of all, and to the spirits of the righteous made perfect, and to Jesus, the mediator of a new covenant, and to the sprinkled blood that speaks a better word than the blood of Abel.
We believe, therefore, since we are receiving a kingdom that cannot be shaken, we are to offer to God an acceptable worship with reverence and awe; for indeed our God is a consuming fire.

Proper 17 (Year C)

Sunday between August 28 and September 3 inclusive

LECTIONARY READINGS

Proverbs 25:6–7
Psalm 112
Hebrews 13:1–8, 15–16
Luke 14:1, 7–14

CALL TO WORSHIP

Psalm 112:1–2

Praise the Lord! Blessed are those who fear the Lord,
who greatly delight in his commandments.
Their descendants will be mighty in the land;
the generation of the upright will be blessed.

PRAYER OF RENEWAL

Based on Psalm 112:1–10

Gracious Lord,
help us to delight in your commandments.
May we rise in the darkness as a light
and be gracious, merciful, and righteous.
We want to be a generous people who conduct their affairs with justice,
and who know the joy of giving to those in need.
Keep us from all fear and evil; may our hearts remain steady, firm, and secure in you. In the name of Jesus we pray. Amen.

AFFIRMATION OF FAITH

Based on Hebrews 13:1–5

What do we believe concerning loving relationships and contentment?

We believe that we are to let mutual love continue.
We believe we should not neglect to show hospitality to strangers.
We believe we are to remember those who are in prison, as though we were in prison with them; those who are being persecuted, as though we ourselves were being persecuted.
We believe marriage is to be held in honor by all, and that the marriage bed should be kept undefiled; for God will judge the sexually immoral and adulterous.
We believe we are to keep our lives free from the love of money,
and be content with what we have.

Proper 18 (Year C)

Sunday between September 4 and September 10 inclusive

LECTIONARY READINGS

Deuteronomy 30:15–20
Psalm 1
Philemon 1–21
Luke 14:25–33

CALL TO WORSHIP

Based on Philemon 3–7

As we join in worship may we receive grace and peace
from God our Father and the Lord Jesus Christ.
May our love for all the saints and our faith toward the Lord Jesus increase.
May we receive joy and encouragement and may our hearts be refreshed.

PRAYER OF RENEWAL

Based on Luke 14:25–33; Deuteronomy 30:15–16, 20

Loving Savior,
may we count the cost of being your disciple,
and be willing to give up all of our possessions to follow you.
Fill us, renew us, and grant us the desire
to choose life and abundance today.
Help us to love you, to walk in your ways,
to observe your commandments,
and to hold fast to you in all circumstances.
In the name of Jesus we pray. Amen.

AFFIRMATION OF FAITH

Based on Psalm 1:1–3

What do we believe concerning the blessings of God?

We believe we are blessed when we do not follow the advice of the wicked, or take the path that sinners tread, or sit in the seat of scoffers;
but our delight is in the law of the Lord, and on his law we meditate day and night.
We believe that when we obey God's ways we are like trees planted by streams of water,
which bear fruit in its season, and whose leaves do not wither.

Proper 19 (Year C)

Sunday between September 11 and September 17 inclusive

LECTIONARY READINGS

Exodus 32:7–14
Psalm 51:1–10
1 Timothy 1:12–17
Luke 15:1–10

CALL TO WORSHIP

1 Timothy 1:17

To the King of the ages, immortal, invisible, the only God,
be honor and glory forever and ever. Amen.

PRAYER OF RENEWAL

Psalm 51:1–2, 6–7, 10

Have mercy on me, O God,
according to your steadfast love;
according to your abundant mercy
blot out my transgressions.
Wash me thoroughly from my iniquity,
and cleanse me from my sin.
You desire truth in the inward being;
therefore teach me wisdom in my secret heart.
Purify me from my sins, and I shall be clean;
wash me, and I shall be whiter than snow.
Create in me a clean heart, O God,
and put a new and right spirit within me.
In the name of Jesus I pray. Amen.

AFFIRMATION OF FAITH

Based on Luke 15:7, 10

What do we believe concerning the repentance of sinners?

We believe there will be more joy in heaven over one sinner who repents than over ninety-nine righteous persons who need no repentance.
We believe there is joy in the presence of the angels of God over one sinner who repents.

Proper 20 (Year C)

Sunday between September 18 and September 24 inclusive

LECTIONARY READINGS

Amos 8:4–7
Psalm 113
1 Timothy 2:1–7
Luke 16:1–13

CALL TO WORSHIP

Psalm 113:1–3

Praise the Lord! Praise, O servants of the Lord; praise the name of the Lord.
Blessed be the name of the Lord from this time on and forevermore.
From the rising of the sun to its setting the name of the Lord is to be praised.

PRAYER OF INTERCESSION

Based on Amos 8:4; Psalm 113:5–7

Merciful God,
help us to treat everyone
with dignity and respect, as fellow image bearers.
May we not trample on the needy,
nor bring to ruin the poor of our towns and cities.
Give us your heart for those in need,
that we may help raise the poor from the dust,
and lift the needy from desperate circumstances.
In the name of Jesus we pray. Amen.

AFFIRMATION OF FAITH

Based on 1 Timothy 2:1–6

What do we believe concerning prayer and the intercessory role of Christ?

We believe that supplications, prayers, intercessions, and thanksgivings
should be made for everyone, for kings and all who are in high positions,
so that we may lead a quiet and peaceable life in all godliness and dignity.
We believe this kind of prayer is right and is acceptable in the sight of God
our Savior,
who desires everyone to be saved and to come to the knowledge of the truth.
We believe there is one God; there is also one mediator between God and
humankind, Christ Jesus, himself human, who gave himself a ransom for all.

Proper 21 (Year C)

Sunday between September 25 and October 1 inclusive

LECTIONARY READINGS

Amos 6:1a, 4–7
Psalm 146
1 Timothy 6:6–19
Luke 16:19–31

CALL TO WORSHIP

Psalm 146:1–2

Praise the Lord, O my soul!
I will praise the Lord as long as I live;
I will sing praises to my God all my life long.

PRAYER OF RENEWAL

Based on Amos 6:1, 6; Psalm 146:3–7; 1 Timothy 6:18–19

Holy God, may our hope be only in you.
Forgive us when we become complacent
and forget your power, your might, and your heart for those in need.
You are the one who made heaven and earth, the sea, and all that is in them.
You keep your promises forever;
you execute justice for the oppressed; and you give food to the hungry.
Help us to be vessels of your grace,
not setting our hearts on the uncertainty of wealth,
but seeking the riches of good works and generosity,
that we may take hold of that which is truly life.
In the name of Jesus we pray. Amen.

AFFIRMATION OF FAITH

Based on 1 Timothy 6:6–8, 10–11, 18–19

What do we believe concerning godliness and contentment?

We believe there is great gain in godliness combined with contentment;
for we brought nothing into the world, so that we can take nothing out of it;
but if we have food and clothing, we will be content with these.
We believe the love of money is a root of all kinds of evil;
thus, we are to pursue righteousness, godliness, faith, love, endurance, and gentleness.
We believe we are to do good, to be rich in good works, generous, and ready to share,
thus storing up for ourselves the treasure of a good foundation for the future,
so that we may take hold of the life that really is life.

Proper 22 (Year C)

Sunday between October 2 and October 8 inclusive

LECTIONARY READINGS

Habakkuk 1:1–4; 2:1–4
Psalm 37:1–9
2 Timothy 1:1–14
Luke 17:5–10

CALL TO WORSHIP

Psalm 37:3–4

Trust in the Lord, and do good;
so you will live in the land, and enjoy security.
Take delight in the Lord, and he will give you the desires of your heart.

PRAYER OF RENEWAL

Based on Habakkuk 2:4; Psalm 37:5–9; Luke 17:6

Sovereign Lord, you tell us that the righteous shall live by faith.
Help us to exercise our faith, however small,
with the assurance that you are able to do
abundantly more than all we could ask or imagine.
May we commit our way to you
and trust that you will act on our behalf.
May we not resent those who prosper through evil means,
but be still before you, waiting patiently
for the greater blessing of your presence and peace.
In the name of Jesus we pray. Amen.

AFFIRMATION OF FAITH

Based on 2 Timothy 1:8–10, 13–14

What do we believe concerning our suffering for and holding to the sound teaching of the gospel?

We believe we should not be ashamed of suffering for the gospel,
but should rely on the power of God, who saved us and called us with a holy calling,
not according to our works but according to his own purpose and grace.
We believe this grace was given to us in Christ Jesus before the ages began,
but it has now been revealed through the appearing of our Savior Christ Jesus,
who abolished death and brought life and immortality to light through the gospel.
We believe we are to hold to the standard of sound teaching that we have in God's word and guard this good news that has been entrusted to us, with the help of the Holy Spirit living in us.

Proper 23 (Year C)

Sunday between October 9 and October 15 inclusive

LECTIONARY READINGS

2 Kings 5:1–3, 7–15c
Psalm 111
2 Timothy 2:8–15
Luke 17:11–19

CALL TO WORSHIP

Psalm 111:1–3

Praise the Lord! I will give thanks to the Lord with my whole heart,
in the company of the upright, in the congregation.
Great are the works of the Lord, studied by all who delight in them.
Full of honor and majesty is his work, and his righteousness endures forever.

PRAYER OF RENEWAL

Based on Psalm 111:7–10; 2 Kings 5:8–15; Luke 17:11–19

Merciful God,
the works of your hands are faithful and just;
all of your commandments are trustworthy.
They are established forever and ever,
to be performed with faithfulness and uprightness.
You sent redemption to your people;
you have commanded your covenant forever.
Holy and awesome is your name.
Give us thankful hearts that respond to all
the ways you bring healing and restoration into our lives.
May we not let pride get in the way of obeying you,

but may our lives reveal that reverence for your name
is the beginning of wisdom and understanding.
In the name of Jesus we pray. Amen.

AFFIRMATION OF FAITH

Based on 2 Timothy 2:11–13

What do we believe concerning our relationship with Jesus?

We believe that if we have died with him,
we will also live with him;
if we endure, we will also reign with him;
if we deny him, he will also deny us;
if we are faithless, he remains faithful—
for he cannot deny himself.

Proper 24 (Year C)

Sunday between October 16 and October 22 inclusive

LECTIONARY READINGS

Genesis 32:22–31
Psalm 121
2 Timothy 3:14–4:5
Luke 18:1–8

CALL TO WORSHIP

Psalm 121:1–2

I lift up my eyes to the hills—
from where will my help come?
**My help comes from the Lord,
who made heaven and earth.**

PRAYER OF RENEWAL

Based on Psalm 121:3–8; Luke 18:1–8

Almighty God,
we can draw near to you at any time in prayer.
Though our lives may be in chaos,
we can rest in knowing that you neither slumber nor sleep.
You are our keeper;
you watch over us day and night.
You keep us from all evil;
you watch over our lives:
our going out and our coming in, now and forever.
In the name of Jesus we pray. Amen.

AFFIRMATION OF FAITH

Based 2 Timothy 3:14–17

What do we believe concerning the instructive nature of God's word?

We believe that God's word is able to instruct us for salvation through faith in Christ Jesus.
We believe that all scripture is inspired by God and is useful for teaching, for reproof, for correction, and for training in righteousness,
so that everyone who belongs to God may be proficient, equipped for every good work.

Proper 25 (Year C)

Sunday between October 23 and October 29 inclusive

LECTIONARY READINGS

Jeremiah 14:7–10, 19–22
Psalm 84:1–7
2 Timothy 4:6–8, 16–18
Luke 18:9–14

CALL TO WORSHIP

Psalm 84:1–2

How lovely is your dwelling place, O Lord of hosts!
My soul longs, indeed it faints for the courts of the Lord;
my heart and my flesh sing for joy to the living God.

PRAYER OF RENEWAL

Based on Luke 18:9–14; Psalm 84:5–7; 2 Timothy 4:7

Gracious Lord,
help us not to think too highly ourselves,
but in our humility confess to you
that we are sinners who need your mercy.
May we find our refuge in strength in you alone.
As we go through the valleys of trial and struggle,
make them a place of springs, renewing the dry ground of our hearts.
When our time for departure comes, like Paul,
may we be able to say that we have fought the good fight,
we have finished the race, we have kept the faith.
In the name of Jesus we pray. Amen.

AFFIRMATION OF FAITH

Based on Luke 18:14

What do we believe concerning pride and humility?

We believe that all who exalt themselves will be humbled,
but all who humble themselves will be exalted.

Proper 26 (Year C)

Sunday between October 30 and November 5 inclusive

LECTIONARY READINGS

Isaiah 1:10–18
Psalm 32:1–7
2 Thessalonians 1:1–4, 11–12
Luke 19:1–10

CALL TO WORSHIP

Psalm 32:7

You are a hiding place for me;
you preserve me from trouble;
you surround me with glad cries of deliverance.

PRAYER OF RENEWAL

Based on Isaiah 1:10–17

Merciful God,
we confess that we can be self-righteous
and full of religious activity, while our hearts are far from you.
Through the power of the Holy Spirit,
may we cease to do evil and learn to do good.
Help us to seek justice, rescue the oppressed,
defend the orphan, and plead for the widow.
In the name of Jesus we pray. Amen.

AFFIRMATION OF FAITH

Based on 2 Thessalonians 1:3–4, 11–12

What do we believe concerning thanksgiving, faith, prayer, and persecution?

We believe that we must always give thanks to God when brothers and sisters are growing abundantly in faith and when their love for one another is increasing.
We believe the church is to exemplify steadfastness
and faith during times of persecution and affliction.
We believe we are to pray and ask that our God will make us worthy of his call and will fulfill by his power every good resolve and work of faith, so that the name of our Lord Jesus may be glorified in us, and we in him, according to the grace of our God and the Lord Jesus Christ.

Proper 27 (Year C)

Sunday between November 6 and November 12 inclusive

LECTIONARY READINGS

Job 19:23–27a
Psalm 17:1–9
2 Thessalonians 2:1–5, 13–17
Luke 20:27–38

CALL TO WORSHIP

Psalm 17:6–7

I call upon you, for you will answer me, O God;
incline your ear to me, hear my words.
Wondrously show your steadfast love,
O savior of those who seek refuge
from their adversaries at your right hand.

PRAYER OF RENEWAL

Based on Psalm 17:8; 2 Thessalonians 2:15, 17; Luke 20:37–38

Lord Jesus,
guard us and hide us in the shadow of your wings.
Help us to stand firm and hold fast
to the truths that we have been taught.
Comfort our hearts and strengthen them in every good work and word.
As your children, who will one day be raised to new life,
may we know you as the God of Abraham,
the God of Isaac, and the God of Jacob—
the God not of the dead, but of the living; for to you all of them are alive.
In the name of Jesus we pray. Amen.

AFFIRMATION OF FAITH

Based on Job 19:25, 27; 2 Thessalonians 2:1–4

What do we believe concerning the coming of the Lord and our being gathered together with him?

We believe that our Redeemer, the Lord Jesus Christ, lives,
and that at the last he will stand upon the earth; and we shall behold him with our eyes.
We believe that the day of the Lord will not come until the rebellion comes first and the lawless one is revealed, the one destined for destruction.
We believe that the lawless one opposes and exalts himself above every so-called god or object of worship, so that he takes his seat in the temple of God, declaring himself to be God.

Proper 28 (Year C)

Sunday between November 13 and November 19 inclusive

LECTIONARY READINGS

Malachi 4:1–2a
Psalm 98
2 Thessalonians 3:6–13
Luke 21:5–19

CALL TO WORSHIP

Psalm 98:4–6

Make a joyful noise to the Lord, all the earth;
break forth into joyous song and sing praises.
Sing praises to the Lord with the lyre,
with the lyre and the sound of melody.
With trumpets and the sound of the horn
make a joyful noise before the King, the Lord.

PRAYER OF INTERCESSION

Based on Malachi 4:1–2; Luke 21:5–19

Sovereign Lord, we know that the day is coming,
when all the arrogant and all evildoers will be no more;
and when all those who revere your name
shall be filled with great joy, finding healing in your wings.
We know that as that day draws near, we will see
nation rise against nation, and kingdom against kingdom;
there will be great earthquakes, and in various places famines and plagues;
and there will be dreadful warnings and great signs from heaven.
May we not be led astray, but stand firm in your truth.
In the name of Jesus we pray. Amen.

AFFIRMATION OF FAITH

Based on 2 Thessalonians 3:6, 12–13

What do we believe concerning hard work and doing what is right?

We believe that we are to keep away from believers who are living in idleness.
We believe we are to work quietly and earn our own living;
not growing weary in doing what is right.

Christ the King (Year C)

LECTIONARY READINGS

Jeremiah 23:1–6
Psalm 46
Colossians 1:11–20
Luke 23:33–43

CALL TO WORSHIP

Psalm 46:1

God is our refuge and strength,
a very present help in trouble.

PRAYER OF ADORATION

Based on Jeremiah 23:5; Luke 23:33–34, 43; Colossians 1:20

Lord Jesus,
you are the righteous Branch, our King.
You rule wisely and execute justice
and righteousness from your throne.
Though you were mocked and crucified,
you interceded on our behalf and prayed:
"Father, forgive them; for they do not know what they are doing."
Like the criminal on the cross, we deserved death,
but in your mercy you made a way for us to be with you in Paradise.
We praise you for being our Redeemer,
the one who has reconciled to yourself all things,
by making peace through the blood of your cross. Amen.

AFFIRMATION OF FAITH

Based on Colossians 1:15–20

What do we believe concerning the preeminence of Christ?

We believe he is the image of the invisible God, the firstborn of all creation; for in him all things in heaven and on earth were created, things visible and invisible, whether thrones or dominions or rulers or powers—all things have been created through him and for him.
We believe he is before all things, and in him all things hold together.
We believe he is the head of the body, the church; he is the beginning, the firstborn from the dead, so that he might come to have first place in everything.
We believe that in him all the fullness of God was pleased to dwell, and through him God was pleased to reconcile to himself all things, whether on earth or in heaven, by making peace through the blood of his cross.

Bibliography

Consultation on Common Texts. *The Revised Common Lectionary*. Minneapolis: Fortress, 2012.

Gardiner, John Eliot. *Bach: Music in the Castle of Heaven*. New York: Random House, 2013.

Green, Joel B., et al. *Connections: A Lectionary Commentary for Preaching and Worship*. Louisville: Westminster John Knox, 2019.

Long, Kimberly Bracken, ed. *Feasting on the Word Worship Companion: Liturgies for Year A, Volume 1*. Louisville: Westminster John Knox, 2013.

Mitman, F. Russell. *Worship in the Shape of Scripture*. Cleveland: Pilgrim, 2001.

Webber, Robert E., ed. *Music and the Arts in Christian Worship*. The Complete Library of Christian Worship Volume 4, Book 1. Peabody, MA: Hendrickson, 1994.

Subject Index

This index will allow you to locate specific topics covered in the affirmations of faith.

accomplishments, earthly, 117
adoption, 95, 147, 195, 225, 281, 339
ancestors, spiritual, 365, 367
apostles, 25, 35, 79, 219, 347
assembly, heavenly, 369

baptism, 175, 361
Baptist, John the
    baptism of, 153
    ministry of, 139, 269, 285
    testimony of, 23, 285
beatitudes, 295
bodies, glorification of our, 195, 309

Christ
    ascension of, 71, 203, 335
    authority of, 275, 359
    baptism of, 21, 285
    birth of, 11, 143, 147, 275
    blood of, 63
    body of, 289
    burial of, 321
    comfort and protection of, 73
    cross of, 25
    death of, 189, 243, 293
    eternal Word, 17, 145, 149
    exaltation of, 115, 317
    foretelling the birth of, 141
    followers of, 49, 107, 113, 233, 235, 239, 243
    generosity of, 221
    high priest, 15, 57, 183, 253, 255
    humiliation of, 115, 317
    identity in, 351
    knowing, 315
    life in, 349, 383
    mediator, 377
    ministry of, 249
    mystery of, 19
    obedience of, 273
    position in, 313, 315
    post-resurrection appearances of, 71, 293, 335
    preeminence of, 337, 395
    relationship with, 383
    resurrection of, 243, 293, 323
    righteousness of, 43
    sacrifice of, 273
    second coming, 3, 127, 129, 135, 137, 195, 259, 263, 267, 291, 299, 325, 337, 343, 391
    servanthood of, 187
    spiritual blessings in, 225
    sufferings of, 65, 243
    testimony of, 201, 205
    transfiguration of, 39, 303
    triumphal entry of, 53, 185
    union with, 87, 155, 165, 349, 383
church, 19, 33, 67, 289, 325, 335
circumcision, 361
citizenship, heavenly, 309
city, holy, 333
commandment, greatest, 123, 357
commission, great, 77

SUBJECT INDEX

contentment, 371, 379
creation, new, 217, 313, 363
cross, message of the, 179

days, last, 261
disciples
    calling of, 157
    sending of, 223

earth, new, 331
evangelists, 31

faith, 83, 119, 177, 365, 367, 389
fasting, 41
fruit of the Spirit, 353

gifts, spiritual, 231, 287, 289
God
    blessings of, 373
    character of, 99, 229
    children of, 339, 351
    household of, 227
    power of, 131
    sovereignty of, 61
    strength and compassion of, 161
    submission to, 245
    temple of, 33
    testimony of, 205
    word of, 125, 251, 357, 385
gospel, 9, 27, 37, 59, 81, 171, 191, 301, 345, 381
glory, eternal, 215
grace, 89, 91, 93, 181, 225, 281, 381

heaven
    assembly of, 369
    new, 331
    vision of, 327
humility, 387

justification, 47, 85

kingdom, 7, 209

law, 247, 357, 373
life, eternal, 209, 329
love, 63, 109, 111, 279, 297, 355, 371

marriage, 371
men, wise, 151, 283
money, love of, 371, 379

persecution, 389
prayer, 41, 97, 271, 377, 389
predestination, 97, 225, 281
pride, 159, 387
promises, 83, 165, 177, 269

religion, pure, 239
repentance, 375
responsibilities, earthly and godly, 121
restoration, 355
revelation, 13, 249, 341

Sabbath, 169, 213
salvation, 45, 63, 101, 173, 175, 209, 277, 307, 361
sanctification, 105, 163
Scripture, 5, 381, 385
Shepherd, Good, 329
sin, 89, 91, 93, 103, 181, 193, 363
Spirit, Holy, 29, 51, 75, 93, 97, 231, 287, 289, 335, 339, 341, 353
suffering, 47, 85, 389
Supper, Lord's, 55, 319

temptation, 311
testimony, 69, 167, 205, 211
testing, 311
treasures, earthly and heavenly, 305, 379

warfare, spiritual, 237
works, good, 181, 241, 379, 393
worship, 105

Zechariah, prophecy of, 269

Scripture Index

Genesis

1:1–2:4a	76
1:1–5	152
2:15–17; 3:1–7	42
2:18–24	248
3:8–15	214
9:8–17	174
12:1–4a	44
15:1–12, 17–18	308
15:1–6	364
17:1–7, 15–16	176
18:1–10a	358
18:20–32	360
32:22–31	384
45:3–11, 15	296
50:15–21	110

Exodus

12:1–14	54, 186, 318
16:2–4, 9–15	230
17:1–7	46
19:2–8a	84
20:1–17	178
24:12–18	38
32:7–14	374
34:29–35	302

Leviticus

19:1–2, 9–18	32
19:1–2, 15–18	122

Numbers

11:4–6, 10–16, 24–29	246
21:4–9	180

Deuteronomy

4:1–2, 6–9	238
5:12–15	168–69, 212–13
6:1–9	256
11:18–21, 26–28	36, 80
18:15–20	158
26:1–11	306
30:9–14	356–57
30:15–20	372

Joshua

5:9–12	312
24:1–2a, 14–18	236

1 Samuel

2:18–20, 26	278
3:1–20	154
16:1–13	48

2 Samuel

7:1–11, 16	140
11:26–12:10, 13–15	348

1 Kings

3:5–12	96
8:22–23, 41–43	300, 344
17:8–16	258
17:17–24	346
19:4–8	232
19:9–18	100
19:15–16, 19–21	352

2 Kings

2:1–12	170
4:42–44	228
5:1–3, 7–15c	382
5:1–14	162

Nehemiah

8:1–3, 5–6, 8–10	288

Job

19:23–27a	390–91
38:1–11	218

Psalm

1	122, 204, 294, 372–73
4	194
8	76, 248, 340
15	26, 238, 358
16	60, 260, 352
17:1–9	390
19	178, 288
19:7–14	246–47
22	56, 188, 320
22:19–28	350
22:23–31	176
22:25–31	198
23	48, 64, 118, 196, 226, 328–29
25:1–10	174, 266, 356
25:1–9	114
26:1–8	106
27	308–9
27:1, 4–9	24
29	20, 152, 208, 284
30	162, 326, 346, 220
31:1–5, 19–24	36, 80
31:1–5, 15–16	66
32	42, 312, 348
32:1–7	388
33:12–22	364
34:1–8	232
34:9–14	234
34:15–22	236
36:5–10	286
37:1–9	380
37:1–11, 39–40	296
40:1–11	22
41	164
43	124
46	394
47	70, 202, 334
49:1–12	362
50:1–6	170
50:7–15	82
51:1–17	40–41, 172, 304
51:1–10	374
54	244
62:5–12	156
63:1–8	310–11
65	92
66:1–9	354
66:8–20	68
67	102
68:1–10, 32–35	72
69:7–18	86
71:1–6	290
72:1–7, 10–14	18, 150, 282
72:1–7, 18–19	4
78:23–29	230
80:1–7, 17–19	8
80:7–15	116
81:1–10	168, 212
82	366
84:1–7	386
85:1–2, 8–13	136
85:8–13	100, 224
86:11–17	94
89:1–4, 15–18	88
90:1–12	128
90:12–17	250
91:1–2, 9–16	306
91:9–16	252
92:1–4, 12–15	216, 298, 342
93	262
95	46
95:1–7a	130
96	10, 142, 274
96:1–13	120
96:1–9	300, 344
97	336
98	12, 144, 200, 276, 392
99	302
100	84

103:1–13, 22	166, 210	5:1–7	116
103:1–13	110	6:1–13	292
103:1–8	368	6:1–8	208
104:24–34, 35b	74, 206, 338	7:10–16	8
107:1–3, 17–22	180	9:1–4	24
107:1–3, 23–32	218	9:2–7	10, 142, 274–75
111	158, 382	11:1–10	4
112	370	12:2–6	270
112:1–10	28	25:1–9	118
113	376	35:1–10	6–7
116:1–4, 12–19	62	35:4–7a	240
116:1–2, 12–19	54, 186, 318	40:1–11	136
116:1–9	242	40:21–31	160–61
118:1–2, 14–24	58, 190, 322	42:1–9	20
118:1–2, 19–29	52, 184, 316	43:1–7	284
119:1–8	256–57	43:16–21	314
119:33–40	32, 108	43:18–25	164
119:129–136	96	45:1–7	120
121	44, 384	49:1–7	22
122	2	49:8–16a	34, 78
123	222	50:4–9a	242, 316
126	254, 314	51:1–6	104
130	50, 214	52:7–10	12, 144, 276
131	34, 78	52:13–53:12	56–57, 188, 320
133	192	53:4–12	252
138	104, 292, 360	55:1–9	310
139:1–6, 13–18	154	55:1–5	98–99
145:1–8	112	55:10–13	92
145:8–9, 14–21	98–99	56:1, 6–8	102
145:8–14	90	58:1–12	28
145:10–18	228	58:9b–14	368–69
146	240, 258, 378	60:1–6	18, 150, 282
147:1–11, 20	160	60:1–4, 8–11	138
148	14, 146–47, 278, 330	61:10–62:3	146
150	324	62:1–5	286
		63:7–9	14–15
		64:1–9	134

Proverbs

8:1–4, 22–31	340
9:1–6	234

65:1–9	350
66:10–14	354

Ecclesiastes

1:2, 12–14; 2:18–23	362

Jeremiah

1:4–10	290
15:15–21	106
17:5–10	294
20:7–13	86
23:1–6	226, 394
23:23–29	366

Isaiah

1:10–18	388
2:1–5	2

Jeremiah (continued)

28:5–9	88
31:7–9	254
31:31–34	182
33:14–16	266

Ezekiel

2:1–5	222
17:22–24	216
18:1–4, 25–32	114
33:7–11	108
34:11–16, 20–24	130
37:1–14	50

Daniel

7:9–10, 13–14	262–63
12:1–3	260–61

Hosea

2:14–20	166, 210
5:15–6:6	82

Amos

5:6–7, 10–15	250–51
6:1a, 4–7	378
7:7–15	224
8:4–7	376

Jonah

3:1–5, 10	156
3:10–4:11	112

Micah

3:5–12	124
5:2–5a	272
6:1–8	26

Habakkuk

1:1–4; 2:1–4	380

Zephaniah

1:7, 12–18	128
3:14–20	270

Zechariah

9:9–12	90

Malachi

4:1–2a	392

Matthew

1:18–25	8
2:1–12	18, 150–51, 282–83
2:13–23	14–15
3:1–12	4
3:13–17	20–21
4:1–11	42
4:12–23	24
5:1–12	26
5:13–20	28
5:21–37	30–31
5:38–48	32
6:1–6, 16–21	40–41, 172–73, 304–5
6:24–34	34, 78
7:21–29	36–37, 80–81
9:9–13, 18–26	82
9:35–10:23	84
10:24–39	86
10:40–42	88
11:2–11	6
11:16–19, 25–30	90
13:1–9, 18–23	92
13:24–30, 36–43	94
13:31–33, 44–52	96
14:13–21	98–99
14:22–33	100
15:10–28	102–3
16:13–20	104
16:21–28	106
17:1–9	38–39
18:15–20	108
18:21–35	110
20:1–16	112
21:1–11	52–53
21:23–32	114
21:33–46	116
22:1–14	118
22:15–22	120–21
22:34–46	122–23

23:1–12	124	2:1–20	10–11, 142–43, 274
24:36–44	2	2:22–40	146–47
25:1–13	126	2:41–52	278
25:14–30	128	3:1–6	268
25:31–46	130	3:7–18	270
28:16–20	76–77	3:15–17, 21–22	284–85
		4:1–13	306
Mark		4:14–21	288
		4:21–30	290
1:1–8	136	5:1–11	292
1:4–11	152–53	6:17–26	294–95
1:9–15	174	6:27–38	296–97
1:14–20	156–57	6:39–49	298
1:21–28	158	7:1–10	300, 344
1:29–39	160–61	7:11–17	346
1:40–45	162	7:36–8:3	348
2:1–12	164–65	8:26–39	350
2:13–22	166, 210	9:28–43a	302–3
2:23–3:6	168–69, 212–13	9:51–62	352
3:20–35	214	10:1–11, 16–20	354–55
4:26–34	216–17	10:25–37	356–57
4:35–41	218	10:38–42	358
5:21–43	220–21	11:1–13	360
6:1–13	222–23	12:13–21	362
6:14–29	224	12:32–40	364
6:30–34, 53–56	226	12:49–56	366
7:1–8, 14–15, 21–23		13:1–9	310
	238	13:10–17	368
7:24–37	240	14:1, 7–14	370
8:27–38	242–43	14:25–33	372
9:2–9	170	15:1–3, 11b32	312
9:30–37	244	15:1–10	374–75
9:38–50	246	16:1–13	376
10:2–16	248	16:19–31	378
10:17–31	250	17:5–10	380
10:35–45	252	17:11–19	382–83
10:46–52	254	18:1–8	384
11:1–11	184–85	18:9–14	386–87
12:28–34	256–57	19:1–10	388
12:38–44	258–59	19:28–40	316
13:1–8	260	20:27–38	390
13:24–37	134–35	21:5–19	392
		21:25–36	266–67
Luke		23:33–43	394
		24:13–35	62
1:26–38	140–41	24:36b-48	194
1:39–55	272–73	24:44–53	70, 202, 334
1:68–79	268–69		

John

1:1-14	12-13, 144-45, 276-77
1:6-8, 19-28	138-39
1:29-42	22-23
1:43-51	154-55
2:1-11	286
2:13-22	178
3:1-17	208-9
3:14-21	180
4:5-42	46
6:1-21	228
6:24-35	230
6:35, 41-51	232
6:51-58	234
6:56-69	236
9:1-41	48
10:1-10	64
10:11-18	196
10:22-30	328-29
11:1-45	50
12:1-8	314
12:20-33	182
13:1-17, 31b-35	54-55, 186-87, 318
13:31-55	330
14:1-14	66
14:8-17, 25-27	338
14:15-21	68
15:1-8	198
15:9-17	200
15:26-27; 16:4b-15	206
16:12-15	340-41
17:1-11	72
17:6-19	204
17:20-26	336-37
18:1-19:42	56, 188-89, 320-21
18:33-37	262
20:19-31	60, 192, 324
21:1-19	326

Acts

1:1-11	70-71, 202-3, 334-35
1:6-14	72
1:15-17, 21-26	204
2:14a, 22-32	60-61
2:14a, 36-41	62
2:42-47	64
3:12-19	194
4:5-12	196
4:32-35	192
5:27-32	324
7:55-60	66
8:14-17	284
8:26-40	198
9:1-20	326
9:36-43	328
10:34-43	20
10:44-48	200
11:1-18	330
16:9-15	332
16:16-34	336
17:22-31	68
19:1-7	152-53

Romans

1:1-7	8-9
1:16-17; 3:22b-31	36-37, 80-81
4:1-5, 13-17	44
4:13-25	82-83, 176-77
5:1-11	46-47
5:1-8	84-85
5:1-5	340
5:12-19	42-43
6:1b-11	86-87
6:12-23	88-89
7:15-25a	90-91
8:1-11	92-93
8:6-11	50-51
8:12-25	94-95
8:12-17	208
8:26-39	96-97
9:1-5	98
10:5-15	100-1
10:8b-13	306-7
11:1-2a, 29-32	102
12:1-8	104-5
12:9-21	106-7
13:8-14	108-9
13:11-14	2-3
14:1-12	110-11
15:4-13	4-5
16:25-27	140

SCRIPTURE INDEX   407

1 Corinthians

1:1–9	22
1:3–9	134–35
1:10–18	24–25
1:18–31	26–27
1:18–25	178–79
2:1–16	28–29
3:1–9	30–31
3:10–11, 16–23	32–33
4:1–5	34–35
6:12–20	154–55
7:29–31	156
8:1–13	158–59
9:16–23	160
9:24–27	162–63
10:1–13	310–11
12:1–11	286–87
12:12–31a	388–89
13:1–13	290–91
15:1–11	292–93
15:12–20	294
15:35–38, 42–50	296
15:51–58	298–99, 342–43

2 Corinthians

1:18–22	164–65
3:1–6	166–67, 210–11
3:12–4:2	302
4:3–6	170–71
4:5–12	168, 212
4:13–5:1	214–15
5:6–17	216–17
5:16–21	312–13
5:20b–6:10	40, 172–73, 304–5
6:1–13	218–19
8:7–15	220–21
12:2–10	222
13:11–13	76–77

Galatians

1:1–12	300–1, 344–45
1:11–24	346–47
2:15–21	348–49
3:23–29	350–51
4:4–7	146–47
5:1, 13–25	352–53
6:1–16	354–55

Ephesians

1:3–14	224–25
1:15–23	70, 130–31, 202, 334
2:1–10	180–81
2:11–22	226–27
3:1–12	18–19, 150, 282
3:14–21	228–29
4:1–16	230–31
4:25–5:2	232–33
5:8–14	48–49
5:15–20	234–35
6:10–20	236–37

Philippians

1:3–11	268
1:21–30	112–13
2:1–13	114–15
2:5–11	316–17
3:4b–14	116–17, 314–15
3:17–41	308–9
4:1–9	118–19
4:4–7	270–71

Colossians

1:1–14	356–57
1:11–20	394–95
1:15–28	358–59
2:6–19	360–61
3:1–11	362–63
3:12–17	278–79

1 Thessalonians

1:1–10	120
2:1–8	122
2:9–13	124–25
3:9–13	266
4:13–18	126–27
5:1–11	128–29
5:16–24	138

2 Thessalonians

1:1–4, 11–12	388–89
2:1–5, 13–17	390–91

2 Thessalonians (continued)

3:6–13	392–93

1 Timothy

1:12–17	374
2:1–7	376–77
6:6–19	378–79

2 Timothy

1:1–14	380–81
2:8–15	382–83
3:14–4:5	384–85
4:6–8, 16–18	386

Titus

2:11–14	10–11, 142, 274

Philemon

1–21	372

Hebrews

1:1–12	12–13, 144, 276
1:1–4; 2:5–12	248–49
2:10–18	14–15
4:12–16	250–51
5:1–10	252–53
5:5–10	182–83
7:23–28	254–55
9:11–14	256
9:24–28	258–59
10:5–10	272–73
10:11–25	260
11:1–3, 8–16	364–65
11:29–12:2	366–67
12:18–29	368–69
13:1–8, 15–16	370–71

James

1:17–27	238–39
2:1–17	240–41
3:1–12	242
3:13–4:3, 7–8a	244–45
5:7–10	6
5:13–20	246

1 Peter

1:3–9	60–61
1:17–23	62–63
2:2–10	66–67
2:19–25	64–65
3:13–22	68–69
3:18–22	174–75
4:12–14; 5:6–11	72–73

2 Peter

1:16–21	38
3:8–15a	136–37

1 John

1:1–2:2	192–93
3:1–7	194–95
3:16–24	196–97
4:7–21	198–99
5:1–6	200–1
5:9–13	204–5

Revelation

1:4–8	324–25
1:4b–8	262–63
5:11–14	326–27
7:9–17	328
21:1–6	330–31
21:10, 21:22–22:5	332–33
22:12–17, 20–21	336–37